I0486513

It's A Long Journey To The Brass Ring
(and that ain't no bologna)

Ken Rich

National Library of Canada Cataloguing in Publication

Rich, Ken, 1945-
    It's a long journey to the brass ring : and that ain't no bologna / Ken Rich.
ISBN 1-4120-0010-6
    1. Success in business.   I. Title.
HF5386.5.R52 2003   650.1
C2003-901233-6

TRAFFORD

This book was published *on-demand* in cooperation with Trafford Publishing. On-demand publishing is a unique process and service of making a book available for retail sale to the public taking advantage of on-demand manufacturing and Internet marketing. **On-demand publishing** includes promotions, retail sales, manufacturing, order fulfilment, accounting and collecting royalties on behalf of the author.

Suite 6E, 2333 Government St., Victoria, B.C. V8T 4P4, CANADA

Phone	250-383-6864	Toll-free	1-888-232-4444 (Canada & US)
Fax	250-383-6804	E-mail	sales@trafford.com
Web site	www.trafford.com	TRAFFORD PUBLISHING IS A DIVISION OF TRAFFORD

HOLDINGS LTD.

Trafford Catalogue #03-0372   www.trafford.com/robots/03-0372.html

10   9   8   7   6   5   4   3   2   1

Acknowledgements

I would like to thank my sister and brother-in-law for their encouragement and the inspiration to author a book. I would also like to thank my wife for her diligence in typing, relentless editing, proofreading, and support in this endeavor. I would like to thank the rest of my family for their love and support throughout the years.

Prologue

Beginning at birth where he "must have been born with a mustache because everyone said that Mother was tickled to death" to enduring his youthful years through grade school and high school at which point he begins to recognize the differences in people, Brent takes you through a story of recognizing those born with a "silver spoon" and being the recipients of great rewards. Unlike he, who worked hard and always seemed to experience the blue-collar jobs and working for those "privileged few".

Brent takes you through his life experiences as a youth and dating, dreams of growing up, where he comes from, and where he wants to be. He eventually enters the corporate world and learns to deal with the unfair situations of "preferential treatment", something he recognized in his early years of grade school. Overcoming these obstacles, primarily "people", he rises to the top of his profession only to be shot back to "Ground Zero".

He continues to dream of success and wealth as he ponders away the days in humorous attempts to just get through the day. At the end, he retires only to find the stock market drop 90%! Success just wasn't his to be had, but as he reflects back through his life he recognizes what he did wrong and translates that information to those reading this book to ensure their success and wealth in life.

It's A Long Journey To The Brass Ring
(and that ain't no bologna)

Chapter 1

As I woke up this morning I opened the drapes, looked out of the window and realized that the front yard looks the same today as it did yesterday. I am fifty-seven years forward from birth, or five score and seven years... looks to me like I may live another thirty years. While sitting here sipping coffee I am watching CNBC to see if the stock market is going to be up today, or in the bunker. My name is Brent Johnson. I am retired from a large aircraft company in Seattle. I rarely have anything to do except for what I can dream up, or pretend I would like to do.

Knowing that my education is three arrows short of a full quiver, I still have thoughts and ideas that would confuse the minds of some scholars. To believe that I am an "individual", I would have to believe that I am different from others. It may be true that my life has been spent thinking and dreaming of things that could be. These ideas started in a small, remote place on the map called Bitterwater.

I have spent my entire life providing for myself as well as others while pursuing the brass ring. Subsistence is difficult to acquire, but grasping the brass ring is even more difficult. I learned at a very young age that in order to reap the rewards of the brass ring you must either be born of parents that possess power and influence, or work very hard and be extremely lucky. If your parents possess power and influence, you too will be thrust into the rewards of the "privileged few". These rewards begin early in life. If your parents are members of the school board, your grades will be guaranteed to bolster to the inflationary level of unearned accomplishments. This early reward is the catalyst that will continue to provide you with the necessary confidence to succeed throughout your life and will also give you the belief that you are superior to that of other people. The origin of your parent's influence doesn't matter. It could be from political, educational, or business backgrounds. The bottom line is that your parents and their friends must be upper class people. Even the not so privileged will perceive you as something better than they themselves could ever become. I spent thirty-five years of my working life attempting to coordinate a common relationship with the "privileged" in power.

You must have power and influence to propel yourself to extraordinary expectations. If you ever get the preconception of assumption that all you will ever need in life is the "desire" to be successful, and that with an ample amount of hard work you can rocket yourself to the grandeur of wealth and position then you had better think twice. The obstacles are people and to overcome these obstacles you must understand how to manipulate and influence the thoughts of anyone in control of your future. The brass ring is there for the taking, but many "privileged" will try to divert you and give it to someone else. My story is about what to do and what not to do and tells a tale of why some make it and others fail.

Now let's get back to where my perceptions and understandings were first incubated. It was that little, remote spot on the map that was almost not shown called Bitterwater.

Bitterwater is not a city nor is it a town. It is not a township nor is it a community. Bitterwater is more like a miniscule freckle on the ass of a non-prolific endangered species.

This place included five houses resembling quintuplets with no differentiating characteristics, or variance to personality. I always believed that our house was the "flagship" of the regatta. This freckle was placed in a location where in any direction one might journey, civilization would be in the opposite.

Bitterwater was constructed in 1933 in an arid and desolate valley. The circumferential view would disclose the framing of rolling hills absent of any trees or green foliage. The reflections of the wind blown wheat fields while glistening in the sunlight were not unlike that of the waving actions of a distant south sea. The bottomland, being gently sloped, was covered with yellow ryegrass and gray sagebrush. It had a small, meandering dry-creek bed that would flow water only during the nourishing rainfalls of winter. The desert-like environment could be extremely hot in the summer, but rarely cold in the winter. Snow was something we dreamed of at Christmas time, but only once in my childhood was I able to observe the white ice painting the dry rolling terrains.

As viewed in the family picture of the five siblings I would be second from the youngest. I was born the year of the notorious atom bomb – 1945. "Happy days are here again!"

In order to explain how I got to Bitterwater, I need to tell you of times passed prior to my birth. As the stories have been told to me and handed down, my thoughts of Mother and Dad are as follows:

Both of my parents were born and raised in the farm belt in the southern state of Texas. Mother grew up in the small, quiet town of Muleshoe. Her loving father was engaged in the residential and commercial sales of real estate. Although they were not members of the "privileged few", this life was better for them than most others living there in that place and time. Dad grew up near the small, non-industrialized town of Bailyburr. Dad's life was more challenging than that of others. He and his father were struggling sharecroppers. (This meant farming someone else's land and sharing in the reap of the harvest.)

Mother and Dad were married during "The Great Depression". They had two children: my older sister, Pukette, and my older brother, John. Dad worked hard as a sharecropper trying to seek out a meager existence. Sharecropping was tougher than most people of today could possibly imagine. Money was always tight and luxuries were rare for them.

By 1941, the Japanese had attacked Pearl Harbor, the beginning of World War II. Because of the war, jobs started opening up in the big cities.

My mother's older brother, Uncle Harding, was already living in Mojave, California and working in the local gold mine. Uncle Harding was doing much better than he had done in Texas and he wanted to share this opportunity with Mother and Dad. After encouraging them to make a total life-altering change, Mom and Dad mustered up enough courage to give up the security of their endless poverty and move westward seeking the hope of a more prosperous life. "There's gold in them there hills."

Displaying a mattress strapped to the top of his old Model T Ford, Dad, Mother, and the kids became contributing members of the westward migration. Dad immediately landed a job for the same gold mine that employed Uncle Harding. The family moved into a railroad boxcar that was provided by the mining company and sat just a few feet away from the company. There were no windows, one giant sliding door, and it was insufferably hot! The temperature in Mojave, being that it is in the desert, is 110 degrees in the summer! It is ALWAYS summer in Mojave! Dad is lucky because his new job didn't require him to be exposed to the relentless blistering sunlight as he had been accustomed during his sharecropping days of farming. This new job was working in the relentless darkness of a deep underground mine. Dad was in excellent physical condition, as he was in his early twenties, so he was given the position of running the backbreaking steam drill. He would run that steam drill ten hours a day while beads of sweat would fall from his brow. The country boy was enthusiastic and the straw boss was impressed with his stamina. The workers would often times hold competitions as to who could drill the fastest hole in the ore concealing bedrock. Those holes were drilled to allow the demolition boys a place to store the dynamite charges that would blast the ore from the guts of the mine. Dad worked the gold mine for an extended period of time and never saw one glittering gold nugget! The mine was low-grade and it would require many tons of ore to be extracted just to produce one ounce of gold dust! This story of Dad working in the gold mine reminds me of the famous old-time miner John Henry, the steel driving man.

By this time the big war, World War II, was in full swing. This was the "war to end all wars!" (Harry Truman, 1943.) All of the available single men and volunteers were in the service of Uncle Sam. This military build up would create a shortage of available labor on the home front. The best jobs would be to buil;d the necessary hardware required to fight the war.

Mother, Dad, kids, Uncle Harding, & Aunt Macy will leave the "Glory Hole" and move to the big, fast, moving city of Los Angeles. "Go West Young Man...Go West." (Horace Greely.)

Upon arriving in L.A., Dad applied for work and was quickly hired as a boilermaker at the Navy Shipyards of Gardena. Dad worked this job as long as he could tolerate. Within one year of working on the new job, he could no longer accept the feeling of guilt that encompassed his thoughts. He didn't feel comfortable walking the streets of Gardena during the war with many people looking at him as if to say, "You must be 4-F!" (Unfit for service.) Dad decided it was time to involve himself in the war and confront the "Japs", better known today as the "Japanese".

Dad had a deferment from military service because of his critical job building the Navy ships necessary to continue the war effort. As important and contributing as this job was, he still felt the agonizing need to participate in the actual winning of the war. He was no draft dodger. He was no coward. He was a real cowboy. Even though Dad had just become the proud father of his third child, Alvis, the time had now come for him to sacrifice his easy life and give his all to defend the United States of America.

Soon Dad would say goodbye to his loving family and headed off to see the world through a porthole. With his new Navy job as "Seaman First Class" he would now realize that the porthole view would be a look into the death defying bowels of hell! Unlike today in peacetime, this venture would not be like a safe walk in the park. Dad made the journey across the Pacific Ocean with three thousand ready to kill, "red-neck" Marines. He would later learn that secret destination of the West bound ship. They were heading for a small, enemy inhabited island in the Western Pacific Ocean called Okinawa. He would now be in the middle of the war! The island was still occupied by one hundred thousand Japanese soldiers.

Dad was now titled a "Navy Sea-Bee". He was assigned a job that would fit the work experience that he had gained while farming in the desolate country of Texas. This meant that he would be driving a tractor! The Sea Bees were brought to the small island to build a strategic airstrip necessary for the allied Air Forces to land planes that would bring in troops and supplies. Each day the "Texas Sharecropper" would drive his tractor down and back along the airstrip. The airstrip could have been built in five days, but Dad worked on it for eighteen months. As fast as the Sea-Bees' could build the airstrip, the Jap Zeros' would fly over and drop bombs on the field. This would create huge craters in the middle of the runway. Between attacks, Dad's job was to fill the craters and keep the runway open. Just the thought sends chills down my spine! "I love napalm in the morning. It smells like victory!" (Robert Duval, Apocalypse Now.)

Dad never talked much about the war as did many

other Veterans that saw combat and death. To this day I don't think that Dad ever got over the war. I believe that he was affected as were others that had fought in the war. I can't help but think as I sit here and write about Dad in World War II: "This country is now considering going to war in the Middle East. My God! Have people forgotten the tragedies of war and death? This is not a game because the pain will be real and the dead will be dead! Let the people that want war go and fight them!" (Ken Rich, 2002.)

I remember one story in particular that Dad would tell us. It was about sniper fire (bullets) hitting the tractor as he drove along the airstrip. He witnessed the death of a young sailor just a mere seventeen years of age. The unfortunate sailor, while sitting next to Dad, was learning the technical aspects of how to operate this huge piece of machinery. What a tragedy! Dad must have been devastated!

As Dad continued fighting the war we should not forget that Mother is now home alone to care for and raise the children. Mother was having an extremely tough time managing the household and paying the bills. The Navy pay that Dad earned fell far short of the family needs, but Mother had a past of being tough. Showing true grit, she marched to the shipyard where Dad had previously worked and applied for a job. In those historic days, many women replaced the absent men that had gone off to the war. After making arrangements for a responsible person to baby-sit her precious children, Mother would report to the big shipyard for work! It was the first Company job that Mother had since marrying Dad. She was not only smart, but she was also an extremely hard worker! The Company Manager was so impressed with her performance that she was quickly promoted. They would teach her to install pipes throughout the ships. In essence, she became "Rosey the Plumber"!

   As Mother continued working as "Rosey the Plumber", she could not help but feel the growing pumpkin within her. The pumpkin that was growing was going to be me! "God save the world!" After a few months Mother realized, as did the Company, that she was no longer be fit for employment. To maintain the moral standards of the time pregnant women, once they started to "show", would stay home and keep out of public view.

   By now Uncle Harding, being the entrepreneur that he was, had moved to the town of Bakersfield, California. (Buck Owens and Merle Haggard.) Uncle Harding was now a tradesman. This new endeavor would encompass the skill of building homes. He had chosen the laborious job of being a sheet rocker, commonly known as a lather. With the war winding down, troops were beginning to come home and housing was in big demand.

   Now that Mother was alone, pregnant, and absent of job in Gardena she embraced the love of her brother. She will now pack bologna sandwiches and move her family to the city of Bakersfield. Soon the big event would happen. Labor pains started and the "pumpkin" would soon arrive. I was born in Mrs. Frye's maternity home in Oildale, a suburb of Bakersfield. "What a relief it is! I AM NOW HERE!" After counting all of my toes and fingers, I realized that I was probably normal! I must have been born with a mustache because everyone said that Mother was tickled to death!

Now with the war finally over, Dad was on his way home. Dad returned a War Veteran and a hero. This was the first time he and I had ever met – I was ten months old. Dad could not get over how much I resembled him. I am now his favorite too! (Mother and Dad would have to share me!) Dad's coming home would mean that things would change and we would now have a new "chief". Mother was tough, but Dad was tougher!

My father, after having served his country as a Navy Sea Bee, returned to civilian employment. He was hired by a large oil company that owned and operated an oil pipeline which flowed from the oil fields of Central California westward to the Pacific Coast. Bitterwater was a pumping station that forced the oil through the lines to the coast. This pump station is what would bring the family to the place called Bitterwater.

Except for our four neighbors in the Bitterwater compound, the other nearest neighbor lived seven miles down the road. These people were cattle ranchers. They owned all of the land surrounding us within ten miles. Until the pump station was installed at Bitterwater, there were only two classes of people in the valley: ranchers, or people who worked for ranchers. They didn't know if we were upper or lower class. I didn't know this until I was forty!

Chapter 2

With the birth of Mother and Dad's fifth and final
child, my younger sister, Elizabeth, was born. She would
become the "little princess" in the family. The family
was now complete.

Dad was a poor representative of a disciple of God.
He thought that attending church would not fit into his
demanding schedule. However, Mother had no plans of
raising her offspring without ensuing in them the threat
of going to Hell! There were no organized churches
anywhere near Bitterwater, but thanks to the good
people of the valley, a makeshift place was set up every
three weeks to "beam in God". I suspect that this place
of worship was run by "holy rollers".

On the third Sunday, Mother dressed her five children
in every hand-me-down suit and dress that she could
find tucked away in the backroom closet. We all headed
up the little road to meet God. I just couldn't wait! We
arrived at church dressed to a tee. We all looked like
new pennies. Dad stayed home to "watch the place".
After being seated on the folding chairs, the preacher
started screaming. I was only five years old and the
atmosphere was fearful. I looked around and noticed
that everyone had their heads down with their eyes shut.
I just watched. Soon the preacher had completed what I
later learned was "the sermon" and we all went outside.
Mother was proud! She was so proud that she couldn't
pass up the opportunity to accept the offer from an old

farmer toting a camera. The old man said, "Line up and face the sun." We did and the picture will become indented into the history of the Johnson family. About a week later the picture showed up in the mail and Mother was thrilled. Here was her beautiful flock. Being taken in the bright morning sunlight at church, I looked at the picture and at that very moment I could see that there must have been a "Chinaman" in the woodpile of Grandma's past! We were squinting at the bright sunlight and we could have all passed as Chinese. To this day all of my sibling's offspring, as well as mine, show these signs in appearance!?!

I learned to ride a bicycle at age five and loved girls by age six. There were no girls where I lived, but when visiting relatives there were usually some there. Even though the girls I saw were my cousins, they still looked good to me!

Today is my first day of school. I must have been very smart...I had skipped kindergarten! I will now attempt to learn the "Three-R's: reading, writing and arithmetic!" (as quoted by Dad.) After years of watching my older siblings catch the bus to school, I just couldn't wait to start my education. Monday at last and we all grabbed our bologna sandwiches and headed for the bus. I knew my life had just begun!

The schoolhouse was located nine miles down the county road and the bus ride seemed like it would never end. As we pulled into the school parking lot I could see swings, teeter totters, and monkey bars everywhere. There was even a huge play field with a baseball diamond. It appears to me like school is going to be great fun!

When the bell rang, classes started and the fun stopped! I was assigned a desk in the front row. The teacher, Mrs. Nuisance, started walking down the rows of desks and began passing out books and paper. I was so excited that I realized I now had to go to the bathroom! Trying to be prim and proper…as taught by my mother…I raised my hand to gain the attention of the beautiful Mrs. Nuisance. She stopped momentarily and impatiently asked, "What do you want?" I explained to her that I needed to drain my lizard. I don't think Mrs. Nuisance had a clue what I was talking about. She asked me why I had brought a pet to school! As confused as I was about what she had asked…and knowing that I had played with my lizard many times…I had never considered it a "pet"! Soon I was off to the restroom. As I approached the restroom door I couldn't help but notice a sheet of paper with a string and pencil attached to the wall. Because I couldn't read yet, I didn't know it said: "Sign Up Sheet". Not knowing what this sign up sheet meant, therefore, not signing my name, I entered the clean, smelling room. There was a sink and a toilet. "Where was the bathtub?" Being properly trained in "lizard control", I lifted the toilet seat and I began executing the "rhythmic dance of the lizard!" Relief at last! With the job complete I closed the lid, washed my hands, and returned to my desk. It didn't take five minutes until I was called to the teacher's desk. I asked, "Yes Mrs. Nuisance, what can I do for you?" She replied that her son Kilroy, a proud eighth grader, had just returned from the restroom and that he had observed a few drops of pee on the seat. Mrs. Nuisance must have believed cleanliness was close to Godliness because in a short time I was handed a bucket containing water and a sponge. I was also given the necessary instructions that would provide me with the knowledge of how to clean a toilet! "Where is Mom now?" With tears in my eyes, I strolled back to the restroom and looked at the toilet seat. I will be damned! There was pee on that seat! I quickly wiped the dew while wondering where it had come from. I, nonetheless, completed the task and humbly returned to my desk. I didn't realize what Kilroy had done to get me into trouble until I was in the second grade. What a piece of crap he was! Now I understood the meaning…"Kilroy was here"!

From grades one through seven, I attended Choice Valley Elementary. This school consisted of one room, one teacher, and only fourteen kids. The only other kid in my grade was a guy by the name of Gary. I recall the last day of school when I was in the 4rth grade when Mrs. Nuisance came to talk to Gary and me. She stated that due to poor academics, one of us would not be going onto the fifth grade. I was devastated and asked, "Does this mean that next year I will still be in the fourth grade?" She replied, "No, Gary will be." I was thrilled! I had no idea that I was doing so well. I ran home to check the mailbox, looking for my scholarship to M.I.T.!

Looking back, I can now remember and appreciate the fun times in grade school. The winters in Bitterwater were mild and snow was a rarity. We did, however, get the occasional rain. Our school ground was not paved, nor was it concrete. Rain would fall and the earth would turn into a huge quagmire of mud. We were not allowed to play outside on those rainy days. To pass the time of indoor recess, Mrs. Nuisance would organize everyone into groups by age. Each group would be given an assignment commensurate with their abilities. My group would learn to knit. My school was way ahead of the times; no stereotyping of boys and girls. By the fourth grade I had acquired the ability to knit socks and beautiful sweaters. We also learned ceramics and other crafts. I thought that someday I would make someone a good housewife!

The school also had the best collection of real authentic Indian artifacts that fascinated me. These artifacts were provided by Mrs. Nuisance and people of the local community. These old relics were found on the surrounding lands throughout the valley. Mrs. Nuisance would often times boast of her bloodline being one-quarter Native American Indian. No one wanted to piss her off for fear of being scalped! Actually, Mrs. Nuisance was a very successful teacher. To manage eight grades simultaneously required a skill few could master. She had taught three generations in the community by age sixty-five.

Most members of the school board were protégés of Mrs. Nuisance. This created an extreme bond between her and the school board members. Familiarity breeds contempt and gives a euphoric sense of power. The school was hers and she made the rules. If you were not an offspring of a school board member, or a close relative, your privileges would be few and achieving fair recognition would be difficult. Some kids would pass with good grades that had yet to learn Math and English. These kids were born with a "silver spoon". I was aware of the nepotism then and became even more aware of it later in life. Most success is based ninety percent upon WHOM you know and only ten percent upon WHAT you know! I have had problems throughout my life learning to accept and cope with this knowledge that I had gained back then.

In the 1950's the most popular play at Bitterwater was "Cowboys and Indians". I spent many hours playing and pretending to be one of the heroes in the television movies. In those days we made most of our toys. These toys included bows & arrows, wooden guns, and slingshots. From age three until I left home we owned riding horses. With our homemade toys and our horses I think that I made a pretty good Indian. Riding bareback on a running horse at full speed while shooting arrows at a make believe enemy created a sense of euphoria. I felt like Geronimo...a real Indian!

Dad was also like a big kid. He would sometimes join us boys at the creek and we would have what we called "mud ball fights". The object was to choose sides, find a spot where the dirt was wet, grab a piece of the mud, and form a ball. It was agreed that no one would form a ball with a hidden rock inside. I never broke the rules...unless I was losing! Prior to the game, we would accumulate up to fifty or sixty of these "grenades". We would hide behind hills of dirt and throw them at each other until someone either got hurt, or we had run out of mud balls. The winner was the one who told the one crying that he was sorry! While Dad didn't really throw mud balls at us, he always enjoyed the contest.

I remember how much I enjoyed playing in my favorite places. It was the dry creek bed down the far pasture where the horses roamed that I liked best. We would dig ledges along the vertical walls of dirt and climb from the bottom to the top. As the ledge continued higher and steeper someone would usually fall from the cliff. These falls would be twenty to thirty feet to the bottom. It was amazing that no one was ever seriously injured.

At that time I took all of this for granted. I never thought of how fortunate we were to have lived such a thrilling, carefree childhood. My adolescence seemed like it would last forever with no thought of ever growing up. However, things started to change. My sister Pukette, got married and left home. My brother, John, joined the Navy. All that was left at home was Alvis, my younger sister Elizabeth, and me. At this point in my life I was very happy. I was very happy because I was almost the oldest kid. I started feeling like I was more than just someone that should "shut up and get out of the way". This was made possible because the only brother left at home was Alvis. He is only eighteen months older than me and I was not concerned that he might kick my ass!

Chapter 3

Remembering back in my early youth I recall that chores had to be done and as a family we would all participate in these necessary tasks. With four other houses in the complex, most of the neighbors kept their yards up in good repair. Our yard seemed to require more upkeep than that of the other neighbors. While Dad did not want to be embarrassed by living in a house that appeared to be vacant, he was determined to keep up with the Jones'. I quickly learned that Dad was not cut out to be a gardener. From that day on, my two brothers and I became the "Three Stooges; Larry, Moe, and Curly!" Dad did not know what weed killer was, but he understood the use of a hoe and shovel. Dad would mark out the plot of yard that each of us three boys was to hoe and rake. Based on age and ability, Dad would figure the size of the plot that he would assign to each of us. I, being the favorite and the youngest boy, was always given the smallest plot! Mother would check on us periodically throughout the day to evaluate what progress we were making. I must have been a much harder worker than Larry and Moe because I usually finished my micro plot first. We knew that if Dad got home from work before we had completed the assignment we would get a lecture of how good a gardener he was when he was a kid. I was just like Dad! Larry and Moe must have been too slow at gardening because when Dad got home they were usually in trouble! I knew at this time that I did not want to get any bigger. This meant that I would get a bigger plot...not unlike Larry and Moe's!

Working for Dad was always a job that we had to do, but it didn't pay anything. If we had any hopes of earning money we knew that we had to complete our jobs with Dad and then stride out to work for someone else who was willing to pay us a bona fide wage. Alvis and my first paying job was at age eleven and ten. We didn't really apply for this job, but one of the local ranchers had stopped by our house in Bitterwater to ask if any kids wanted to earn some money. His name was Stoney. Stoney said that he was looking for some kids that could assist him in removing rocks from his farm field down the road. Dad was at work and Mother was fielding the questions. She stated that her boys were too young for hard labor. Alvis and I were eavesdropping on the conversation and I had decided that I no longer wanted to be a little boy. I wanted to be big! Alvis and I told Mother and Stoney that we were perfect for the assignment! After Dad got home from work he and Mother hashed it out. Dad reminded Mother that he was only eight years old when he started working in the fields. This convinced Mother that we were old enough! The job would pay $1.00 per hour. The following morning it was planned that Stoney would pick us up in his truck and deliver us to the rock pile. I had already been doing the math as to how rich I was going to become in just one month.

The next morning at 6:00 a.m. Mother banged on the bedroom door and Alvis and I jumped out of bed. We quickly got dressed and entered the kitchen for breakfast. We completed eating a bowl of cereal just in the nick of time. Stoney was just pulling into the driveway ready to deliver us to our new job. We were excited! As we were

21

exiting the door, as Mother always did, she handed Avis and me our usual lunch, bologna sandwiches! We loved bologna! We don't think we liked ham because we didn't know what ham was!

When we arrived at the job site I could see a huge field. This field was covered with rocks as far as the eye could see. Stoney was driving his flatbed truck. This truck was capable of hauling four tons per load. Alvis and I would walk along with the slow moving truck and extract boulders one at a time and load them onto the bed. Some of these boulders were so big that Alvis nor I could lift them. That's when Stoney would stop the truck and assist us in loading the heavy huge rocks. Time passed like a lost turtle traveling miles to a forgotten place. It was summer and the temperature had reached 105 degrees! This work was so grueling that we would require constant water and an occasional rest. After approximately two hours had passed, the truck was finally loaded. This meant that Stoney would leave us alone while he went to empty the truck. The truck was equipped with an automatic lifting bed so unloading it for Stoney was no big deal and didn't require our help. Stoney said, "You boys continue picking up rocks and just make piles. I will be back in about thirty minutes." Alvis and I would continue picking up rocks until the truck was completely out of site. When we could no longer see the smoky exhaust coming from the rear of the truck, nor any movement on the far horizon, we would stop work, collapse in the soft dirt, and stare at the sky. We were never able to anticipate the exact time that the truck would return. We always got caught lying on our asses. Stoney must have had it figured out and didn't care because we didn't get fired! The job lasted for two blistering weeks. We were glad it was over. Even though I was now wealthy, I don't believe I could have kept up that pace much longer. I had felt like a prisoner in Folsom Prison doing hard time. Those cons had nothing on me!

Chapter 4

My older sister Pukette, while in high school, was very popular. She was the most beautiful cheerleader that Shandon High ever had. She never had to worry about friends because everyone was her friend. She never had to worry about a date. Every boy in school wanted to date her. I remember when Pukette started "going steady". She was dating the best basketball player on the team. His name was William Randoff. Bill was short, good looking, and kind of reminded me of Marlon Brando. On a non-specific day Mother and Dad had started planning for a big wedding. Pukette and Bill would become "man and wife". I remember that I always liked Bill. He was a tough little guy with a short man's complex, but he was always nice to me. Soon after the wedding, Pukette and "Marlon Brando" had moved to Taft, California. They were gone and we wouldn't see them except for the occasional visit. Three years later Pukette would find herself as a single mom.

As for my big brother John, he was always my hero and he was the person that I wanted to be like. Dad never stopped talking about all of John's accomplishments. John was bigger than life to me. He was the best baseball player that Shandon ever had. He played second base. We never missed a game. The crowds would cheer. I would cheer. It was like watching the World Series. John was so good at baseball that he was able to do the impossible. The impossible was "the triple play"! As he sat on second base the ball was hit. Like a bullet, the ball headed for John. There were runners on first and second bases. The ball flew through the air with the sound similar to that of a speeding bullet. John leaped in the air like a giant green frog with suction cups on the tips of his fingers! The ball slammed into his mitt! As John had captured the ball, he accidentally landed on second base. This meant two outs! Being the seasoned player that he was, he knew to throw it back to first. The first base runner, believing that the ball was headed to the outfield, made a gallant attempt to capture second base. At the speed of light, John quickly extracted the ball from his mitt and fired it to first base. There was no time for the runner to correct his error. He was out!!! This feat, unheard of in High School baseball, made the Los Angeles Times and to this day Mother proudly displays this clipping on her wall of her home. "WHEN will I ever get to be like John?"

As mentioned earlier, John has left for the Navy. I miss him. My hero is off to see the world that I doubt I will ever get to see. The stories come in through Mom and Dad because I'm down the list on any conversations that the long distance phone bill could bare. While lying on the dining room floor and getting one half of the conversation, I try to imagine what "Big Bro" is doing. My interpretation of what is going on is that he is on a big ship. This ship has many jet aircraft and he has a very important job. Upon his return, I later learned that he was a Third Class Petty Officer responsible for refueling F-16's and A-6's on the flight deck of the largest aircraft carrier in the United States Navy, the U.S.S. Forestall. This job was the most dangerous job on earth! With bombs and fuel everywhere, one miscalculated move could result in bombs and fuel exploding causing injury and death of everyone on board.

John, being a highly ranked sailor, was one day offered a job to become a Shore Patrol Policeman, commonly known as S.P. This job was his assignment until he separated from the Navy. John will later become a "Deputy Sheriff".

Looking back, I am now glad that John had left the Navy because the ship that he was on, the U.S.S. Forestall, suffered the fate of the odds. A bomb was accidentally dropped on the deck of the carrier. The plane that was responsible for the event was one that had been piloted by a now famous U.S. Senator, John McCain. The fire killed one hundred and thirty-four sailors and almost sent the majestic Forestall to the bottom of the sea. With perseverance, the highly trained crew was able to extinguish the fire that resulted in saving the majority of the crew and the ship. As I think of this today, I am so glad that "Big Mac" (John) wasn't on the aircraft carrier that day. Years later and remembering the stories of John's adventures while on the aircraft carrier inspired me to encourage my second son, Raymond, to follow in my famous brother and heroic father's footsteps. Raymond joined the Navy. Kind of sounds like the story of the famous "Fighting Sullivan Brothers". (The five brothers manning one gun on one ship and they all died for their country in WWII.)

Chapter 5

One spring day upon Dad's release from the confining chains of work, I knew that something was different. He did not take his usual straight-line path to his cushy reclining chair. Instead, he stopped in the kitchen and was brandishing a wide grin from ear to ear. We were all given the big news that he had just closed the deal on a plot of land. This land would be found high in the Sierra Mountains. He wanted a summer cottage. That weekend we all packed the camping gear in the car and headed for the site. On the trip, Dad never stopped talking about what a great purchase he had just made. His excitement radiated to us and soon we all felt like a part of the dream.

This land was located east of Porterville and was accessed by a narrow winding road. This road seemed to climb to the moon. Upon arrival, we could see many tall, old growth pines towering to the sky. The unobstructed view of the majestic mountain peaks was something to behold. From the cabin site it was a brisk hike down the slopping hill to a small crystal clear stream. This stream teamed of small rainbow trout. Just to sit and watch the fish was fascinating. I felt like a Cheshire cat peering through the glass of a huge fully stocked fish aquarium. "I will fish every day!" As we strolled along the lush, damp grass near the water's edge, we became captured by the serenity and stillness of the green forest that surrounded us. What a contrast to the arid landscape of Bitterwater.

From that day forward, evenings were spent with Mother and Dad sitting at the kitchen table planning for the cabin of their dreams. After weeks of arguing, drawing sketches, and figuring the cost, the time had come to start construction.

To assist in the building of the cabin, Dad contracted with a carpenter. This man, being already in his golden years, no longer required a full time job. His name was Jim. Jim may have been slow and uneducated, but he knew how to build a cabin. Dad's decision to hire Jim as his primary carpenter was mostly influenced by the fact that Jim charged only one half the going fee of a real carpenter. Jim would proceed to start the construction of our new cabin. This mountain lot was one hundred and twenty miles northeast of Bitterwater. Even though it was a three-hour drive to the mountains, every Friday the Johnson family would pack the car and head for the hills to check on Jim's progress.

One evening after Dad had just completed his annual phone call to distant relatives in Texas we were given more exciting news. Our Uncle Wilbur was going to move to Bitterwater and live with us. We were all thrilled…except for Mother! Who is Uncle Wilbur? We soon learned that Uncle Wilbur is Dad's older brother. That was all I needed to know! He must be just like Dad and I can't wait to meet him!

About a week later we jumped into the family car and drove to the big city of Bakersfield. We arrived at the bus depot and started looking for Uncle Wilbur. I noticed a tall, thin man standing at the end of the loading dock next to the station. "My God! He looks just like Dad!" As we moved closer I could not help but notice that he also looked like the old cowboy actor, Randolph Scott. After greetings and hugs we all jumped into the car and headed for Bitterwater. I insisted that Uncle Wilbur sit next to me! On the way home I hung onto every word that Dad and Uncle Wilbur had to say. By the time we got home I was fast asleep.

The next morning we sat down to breakfast. Our family had grown larger by one in just a day. With the bright morning sunlight shining through the kitchen window, I was able to get a much better look at Uncle Wilbur. He now looked shorter and also thinner. When he smiled he displayed a full set of gums! "Holy smokes!" I had never seen a toothless man before! Well, after all, he was my uncle and I loved him!

As the days went by I had enjoyed listening to Dad and Uncle Wilbur talking about the old days in Texas. They would talk about night hunting raccoons on the Brazis River. These hunts included the assistance of ten Blood Hounds. The dogs would chase the coon until the coons' only escape would be to climb a tree. This would excite the dogs to bark. All that was left was for the hunters to follow the sound. Now the coon was caught. I would also hear tales of bare knuckle fighting in a barn with other men. This was a sport and the men were not enemies. In those Texas days a man had to prove his manhood and that could only be determined by which one could whip the other.

While hunting raccoon with dogs appealed to me…bare-knuckle fighting did not!

It wasn't long before Uncle Wilbur and Dad had come up with a secret plan. Mother would not be thrilled about this. My brother and I were not let in on the secret. We did, however, notice that everyday after work Dad and Uncle Wilbur would inconspicuously disappear into the darkness of the root cellar under the house. Alvis and I didn't know what they were up to. That root cellar was a dark and scary place. There were deadly black widow spiders, poisonous rattlesnakes, and disease infected rats looming in the confines of the hidden dungeon. For now Dad's secret will be safe!

One evening Dad and Uncle Wilbur returned from the dungeon with success written all over their snickering, sheepish faces. Everything that night seemed funnier than usual. Dad and Uncle Wilbur were almost giddy. Mother was not laughing. She found no humor in their demeanor, or their snide chuckling. Alvis and I figured that the excitement must somehow be related to the precautious cellar. Later that night after everyone had gone to bed, Alvis and I decided that an inspection of the dark dungeon was in order. We would cautiously embark on the trek down the unsure stairs that led to the depths of the cellar. As we opened the door and entered the room we were embraced by total darkness. The only light we had was a wooden match. As I walked across the floor I felt a silk-like thread drag across my gaunt face. My knees felt weak. I wiped my face and slowly proceeded on into the dungeon. Without warning the door on the cellar slammed shut and the faint light of the match was quickly extinguished! In the black of the darkness I could not see my hand in front of my face. My brother, Alvis, had also vanished! Almost too scared to talk I whispered for Alvis to quickly light another match. Alvis did not answer. He was scared speechless. After waving my arms in search of Alvis, I located him. I grabbed the box of matches from his shivering grasp. Three strikes and you're out! It took four matches before I could relax to the glow of the tiny flickering light. Now that we had gathered our non-assuring composure, Alvis and I noticed a light switch just below two big black widow spiders. Not wanting to touch the switch, we found a small wooden stick on the floor. I quickly grabbed the stick, reached towards the light switch, and flipped it on. We were saved! With the light on the cellar now looked as though it were any other room. Even the spiders seemed to have disappeared. There were no snakes nor were there any rats.

Looking around we noticed a glistening shiny contraption gleaming in one corner of the cellar. With more observation we were able to identify carefully planned spiraling coils of copper pipe protruding upward from a huge black pot. Under the pot there was a glowing electric hot plate. These plates were commonly used for cooking food. "What were Dad and Uncle Wilbur doing?" At the top of the copper coils there was a clear one-gallon glass jug sitting on a shelf. This jug would normally be the container for apple cider, but in this case it was not. Observations revealed approximately two inches of a clear liquid in the bottom of the jug. We didn't have a clue what that contraption was until we noticed six or seven one pint Mason jars sitting on an adjacent shelf. These jars appeared to contain a similar clear liquid. We would now have the opportunity to smell and evaluate the contents. "WOW!" When I smelled the liquid my eyes began to water and my nose began to burn. "This smelled just like booze!" Now, we were no "Sherlock Holmes", but we knew that our elusive dad had just gotten busted! Now that we had deduced the truth, we figured that we had better get our asses out of there because we knew that Dad would not reward our unwelcome curiosities. After that experience we preserved Dad's well kept secret. We never divulged to anyone the secret of the dungeon...not even to Mother!

I will never forget the dark nights that I would lie in my comforting bed and hear the slow methodical screeching of the cellar door opening. The sound reminded me of the television movie, "The Munsters" when "Lurch" would return to his coffin as darkness set in. I was no longer ambivalent of the cellar nor was Alvis. We were never obliged to know for sure who was trekking to the cellar each wiling night, but we suspected, by deduction, that it could be Uncle Wilbur!

On one clear, moonlit night we were able to confirm our suspicion. Uncle Wilbur WAS Lurch! After about a month of the deception and fun for the perpetrators the still mysteriously disappeared and mom stayed! Uncle

Wilbur was hanging by a thread. Dad nor I could possibly understand why my favorite Uncle Wilbur was a problem.

By school out the structure of the cabin was starting to take shape. The cabin, based upon Mom and Dad's carefully construed plans, would be a design that would fit the needs of the Johnson family and any friends that may visit the retreat. This included two stories, a rock fireplace and four bedrooms. The huge deck would provide outdoor room for barbecues and a view of the surrounding mountains.

After hiring the not so square carpenter Jim, Dad knew it was time to hire a crew. Dad wanted a crew that would mind like a whip, follow his weekend orders, and offered cheap labor. This was hard to find. He soon learned that his only options were to do it himself, or hire a crew not unlike Uncle Wilbur, Alvis, and me! After fifteen seconds of deliberation, Dad made a highly calculated decision. He would hire the crew of logical choice. Mother thought that this was probably one of the best ideas Dad ever had. Uncle Wilbur will be gone from Bitterwater for three months. Jim worked for one half price, Alvis and I were free, and Uncle Wilbur could also make enough money to buy a bus ticket back to Texas! This was a good business plan and Mother was smiling now!

Construction was going well. Alvis, Uncle Wilbur, and I were loving the wilderness experience. Mother never felt comfortable with the idea that Alvis and I, at the ages of thirteen and fourteen, should be left alone and feed ourselves. But, after Dad explained that we would be babysat by Uncle Wilbur, Mother agreed while probably thinking that WE were actually doing the babysitting!!!!

With the building crew in place we decided we should have a crew leader. An election was held and we voted Uncle Wilbur "foreman" and Alvis and I would be his helpers. We voted Uncle Wilbur as crew leader because we didn't believe that he had ever learned how to take orders in his whole life. He was an entrepreneur, but had never "entrepreneured" anything. We would use child psychology by putting him in charge and if we would make a suggestion about what he could do to improve his status with Dad, the boss, he would give us the freedom to pursue our own plans…fishing! Uncle Wilbur was probably the best boss I ever had. He would let us sleep in and we could quit work anytime we wanted to go fishing. This was the best job even though it didn't pay anything.

Now that we were finally a honed crew the cabin was nearing completion. The last thing to do was to shingle the roof. Alvis and I figured that a climb up to this height should be left to more agile workers and that the boss, Uncle Wilbur, should stay on the ground. It took two weeks to complete just one side of the roof. The other side was completed in just three days. This is called the "learning curve".

As I think back on the shingling of the roof I remember one day in particular. I was nailing shingles and moving fast because my mind was on everything but building the cabin. I was dreaming about women in bikinis. I could hear the loud talk of the people in the cabin above us where a party was ensuing and the adults were screaming and yelling of sexual activities. This party had been going on for three days and Alvis and I couldn't keep our minds on what we were doing. An occasional peak between the treetops would reveal sparsely clad women and we knew that we would never be invited. As I was approaching the end of one row of shingles I found myself waking up on the ground, lying on my back, gasping for air. I just realized what had happened. Somehow I had managed to fall twenty feet from the roof to the ground! I had landed on my head and neck. The ground was not ground at all…it was solid granite rock! It was amazing that I was not killed. By this time Alvis had hastily climbed down the ladder to ground level and had run to the obvious dead body. He was very concerned and I didn't know what the big deal was. Later, I was able to reconfigure the incident and ponder the danger that I was in. To this day I have never gotten over my fear of heights!

As summer came to an end Uncle Wilbur, with his newfound wealth and a little encouragement from Mother, was able to purchase a bus ticket back to his original stomping grounds and bare knuckle fighting of Texas. Things were going to be back to normal for the Johnson family. Just before he left, Alvis and I voted Uncle Wilbur "Foreman of the Summer". Dad was proud of him and Alvis and I were proud of him too! We would have gotten him a trophy, but how do you properly display, in a festivity mode, a half gallon of Jack Daniels? Alvis and I had to return to our education. We sure missed Uncle Wilbur! I always thought that Uncle Wilbur would have been a great "show and tell" project for school.

Chapter 6

On a non-particular morning I caught the small, yellow school bus for the daily, boring ride to school. I, unlike most days, found myself sitting next to a freckle-faced girl that rode the bus daily. I sat next to her quietly, as usual, and didn't bother her in anyway. Suddenly, I couldn't help from noticing a rare view of the passing field gliding across the bus window. I could see a big bull and a medium sized cow performing the task of making steak! It looked to me like the bull was in charge and the cow was grinning from ear to ear. This was too much to view without organizing some type of an audience. The nearest person to me was the skinny, freckle-faced girl sitting to my right. As I pointed out the window I asked, "Does that look like fun?" She turned left and observed the natural production of making beef. Without any unforeseen warning, she abrasively hauled off and slapped my tender young jaws! The pain was so great that I could hardly hold back the stinging tears in my eyes. That was the last time I ever sat next to that unconcerned bitch!

Now that I am fourteen years old, I realize that to extend my manhood and my lust for women I must possess a car. The only car in the family belonged to my dad except for a pale green, 1950 Chevrolet, two door coupe with four tires that didn't match which sat under the trees covered in bird shit. This car belonged to my older brother, John. John was still in the Navy and his plan upon his return home would be to continue driving the old sex machine and pursue his long lost loves.

After being in the Navy for one year, John was looking forward to coming home for Christmas and being with the family. He was stationed in Norfolk, Virginia which put him three thousand miles away from Bitterwater. He needed a plane ticket to fly to the West Coast, but he had no money. He asked Dad to sell his car and send him the proceeds of the sale so that he could buy an airplane ticket. I overheard one half of the telephone conversation and I decided that that car, covered with bird shit, should be mine! I had worked hauling rocks from an early age and I saved all of the money that I had earned in an old mayonnaise jar.

After Dad had hung up the phone from talking to John I asked, "What is the selling price of John's car?"

He absently responded, "$150 dollars!"

Never dreaming that this car could ever be mine, I asked Dad if I could purchase this vehicle. He said he would sell it for $150 dollars.

I quietly asked, "If I can give you $150 dollars will you sell it to me?"

Believing that no kid at fourteen years old from Bitterwater could possibly have $150 dollars, he chuckled and said, "Yes!"

With a hidden smirk on my face, I went to my bedroom and grabbed the old mayonnaise jar from my dresser drawer. This jar contained every dime I had made in my life. I peeled out all of the $1 dollar bills and coins that almost filled the jar. As I counted the money, I came to the unbelievable realization that I had $150 dollars!

As I grasped the crisp bills and cool coins that had been free of air or moisture, I strutted to the living room where Dad was reclined in his favorite chair. I handed him the money and said, "Here is $150 dollars and Big Brother's car now belongs to me!"

In those days $150 dollars was a lot of money. This was 1958!

Dad did not want me to own the car, but $150 dollars was hard to pass up. As he slowly pushed the money into his front, right pocket I knew the deal was made!

He said, "You can own the car, but you will not be able to drive it for two year because you are only fourteen years old."

I proudly responded, "No problem because Alvis is sixteen and we can travel together!"

Alvis possessed the most wonderful thing that anyone under eighteen years of age could possess. It was called a California Driver's License. This was now OUR ticket to fun and romance! This car allowed us to pursue employment with farmers as far away as twenty miles. It also allowed us to go to the drive-in theatre in Paso Robles and attend the dances at Shandon. Girls...Yeah!!!

Alvis and I always double dated (because I could not drive). Being the grown up that I thought I was, as soon as we were out of sight from the Bitterwater Pump Station, I made Alvis pull over and let me drive. Because the car belonged to me, he never gave me any argument. I drove all the way to the blacktop highway where we thought our chances of seeing a California State Patrolman was probable. I would always pull over and put "Big Alvis" back behind the wheel. We would then continue onto the destination that was the exciting event of the night. The exciting event of the night was to pick up our dates. Of course, we were dating the Andrew cousins!

Everyone in high school would always witness the Johnson boys traveling in that old Chevy. They thought Alvis was cool because he had a cool car. No one believed that that car actually belonged to me. This was something that I kept quiet, but it bugged the hell out of me when I heard it.

As I got older the work I would perform for the local ranchers became less laborious and more technical. I was now fifteen years of age and I wanted to follow the same path as my older brothers. One month prior to school out, the poor kids, like me, would start soliciting ranchers for summer jobs. I worked two summers for the same rancher. While I didn't possess a driver's license this rancher gave me the responsibility of driving heavy equipment. Due to the arid environment and the lack of water, the farmers were growing crops that included only wheat and barley. The crops did not require any moisture to grow except for the annual nine inches of rain that fell the prior winter. The terrain was steep, rolling hills and absent of any trees. Most ranchers farmed many thousands of acres. I was now driving a D-7 Caterpillar tractor. This CAT was necessary for pulling a combine. The combine, known as "the harvester", was huge. In one pass it could cut and thatch a forty-foot wide swath of wheat. I was literally towing a giant lawn mower over steep hills! The hills were so steep that the combine required another operator just to run the wheel-leveling device and control the cutting depth of the header. This was very dangerous work. One mistake by the cat driver (me!) and we could all tip over and roll one half mile down to the bottom of the canyon. I was too young to know the danger, but as I look back there is no way I would do that job again. Luckily, Mother had no idea of the danger!

The rancher that employed me was very nice and always treated me with respect. He was a high standing member of the local Shandon School Board. He had one younger son that I had seen at school, but I had never seen him working in the fields that his father owned. I figured that the kid was so rich that he didn't have to

41

work. Maybe Mother and Dad thought work was too hard for him and might interfere with his schoolwork? The big, tall rancher also had a beautiful daughter that was my age. The daughter and I attended classes together at Shandon High. The ranch girls didn't drive tractor, or work on their daddy's ranch.

While I never dated the daughter, my relationship was so good with her dad that I was allowed to use the shower at their ranch house. Every Saturday after work I would go to the ranch house, get paid, shower, and head for town. One Saturday after work I was heading to the ranch house to shower and change clothes. As I approached the house I could hear laughing that sounded like girls in the backyard. My curiosity overtook me and I found myself peering over the backyard fence. I had no idea that this ranch also included a huge in-ground swimming pool. I was even more shocked to see three girls from my school skinny-dipping. It wasn't long before I was told that her mom and dad were away for the weekend and that I should join them for a swim! Because of my HIGH moral standards and downright fear, it took me one minute to strip my clothes and jump in the pool! After swimming a couple of fast laps, just to show off my Olympic skill, I got the notion that these girls were drunk. Most guys would have thought that this was too good to be true. Every man loves loose women! As the girls started approaching me, I started backing up. I was overwhelmed! I had never seen three naked women in my life before…particularly pursuing me! I had backed up until I was against the swimming pool wall. As I felt my butt cheeks pressed against the concrete wall, I was really starting to feel uncomfortable. At that moment I knew that I had better get my ass out of there because if "Big Daddy" showed up he would kick my ass, call the cops, and I would be spending the next three years in reform school. (That's what happened in those days!) I jumped out of the pool. I ran toward the fence and as I stepped on a wet spot on the concrete I slipped and fell flat on my ass! My head smashed against the concrete and I could see stars. With stars in my eyes I jumped the fence, grabbed my clothes, and headed for my car. As I fumbled with my keys I fired up the engine that quickly jumped to maximum acceleration matching that of my heart. I tore down the windy dirt road like a speeding bullet! The dust cloud behind me erupted like that of the Mount St. Helen's eruption! I dreamed of those girls every night for the next six months! "There ain't nothin' like farming!"

Chapter 7

My first day of high school was quite the experience. In 1958 it was always customary to welcome the new, incoming freshman. These freshman would find out the difference between being a small child and becoming an adult. Even the kids growing up together will not, after this day, see each other as the same. The genders have won and genetics will take over. What excitement this will be for everyone. A part of the wonderful introduction to adulthood will begin on this day. It included the old time ritual of initiation. We will call this "hazing". My older brothers had already gone through the scene years prior so I was aware of the drill. They'll paint my face and then throw me in mud. The teachers were involved and things rarely got out of hand.

I recall one incident when a young, brand new teacher was introduced. His name was Mr. DeWire (Archi). He was a recent graduate from the University of Cal Poly in San Luis Obispo and this was his first teaching assignment. With no experience, it was commonplace for recent graduates to be employed by inferior schools. These schools also provided low pay. Oh well, Archi will teach at Shandon High.

On Archi's first day of school he will not be just an observer like the other teachers, but he will become the "hazed". One of the boys, while wearing his beautiful, corduroy, blue FFA (Future Farmers of America) jacket, yelled for someone to get a rope. The boy's pre-planning went without a hitch. As soon as not, five other boys stepped forward and grabbed Archi. They threw him to the ground. A rope was quickly tied around his neck and looped over a horizontal branch of a huge oak tree. "Hang 'Em High" (Clint Eastwood.) With little pressure applied to the rope, the laughter broke out. It was just a joke! (Ha! Ha!) "Welcome Archi, to Shandon High!" The boys that scared the shit out of Archi didn't get any kind of reprimand. It must have been that "silver spoon" thing!

Now that I am completing puberty, high school is becoming more tolerant. I have actually begun to like some of the teachers and I think they like me. My classes are starting to become more interesting and I am actually learning. The more knowledge one attains, the broader the scope of awareness. I was starting to feel like I had been given mind-expanding drugs. I was becoming interested in the politics of the school and the surrounding community. This would include the pecking order of the teachers and the students.

I was now noticing things like the children of the rich ranchers were all driving brand new cars. (Born with a "silver spoon"!?!) I didn't remember seeing any of them working for their dads, or anyone else for that matter. I was working for their dads! I was not jealous, but I must admit I loved their cars! I noticed that the girls loved them BECAUSE of their cars!

Preferential treatment of some did not go completely

45

unnoticed even in my early years of grade school at Choice Valley. At least ten percent of the high school students were "silver spoon" children of the powerful and influential. I noticed then (as I do now) that even the teachers would succumb to the power of a few. The so-called straight-A students were kids to be reckoned with and the teachers feared them. All of the scholarships were won by the bearers of the spoon. Thinking back, I recall a situation involving female twins. They were not identical in their genes, or brains. One of the twins was extremely bright and probably deserved every award she had received. However, the other twin was a little slow and academically challenged. Nonetheless, and as normal protocol would have it, both girls in their senior year were winners of full scholarships to UCLA. Their parents just happened to be on the school board and everyone in the community knew that they were the wealthiest family in the county.

   The preferred treatment was not limited to scholarships or grades for the elite. Absenteeism as well as vandalism was tolerated! I remember that the crimes of the lower classed students never went unpunished. Sometimes I was not able to keep my opinions to myself. I would often walk into the principal's office and demand his utmost attention. I would explain to him that I was from the Bitterwater Valley and I had already felt the wickedness of discrimination. I felt like any black kid might have felt growing up in Dixie! I began to say to the principal, "You see sir, I am aware of your fear. The school board hired you and they can also fire you. The way I see it, we are both in the same boat! To succeed you had better know your place and kiss up."

At the time, I knew he agreed with me, but I was always thrown out of his office. He liked me, as did all of the teachers. I only said what they were all thinking. It depressed me to see my role models act like sheep! Learning about the nature of people at an early age has allowed me to survive and prosper in my later years.

I played all sports in high school lettering in football, basketball, and baseball. I was not a particularly good athlete, but Shandon High School only boasted sixty-three in the entire student body. We played six-man football. We didn't have enough players to play eleven-man. If you could report to play the sport you got a letter in it. Shandon, like Mayberry, had everything except Professor Harold Hill. (The Music Man.)

I did much better in baseball than I did any other sport. However, my passion was football. Anyone who has ever played football knows that it is a full contact sport with rules, a clock, and referees. It is a war! The first time I actually played in a game was an experience I will never forget. Just before the first kick off of my career I could see the opposing team snorting down the field ready to crush us like bugs on a windshield. My knees weakened and my stomach was building with acid. I was almost ready. The whistle sounded and the ball was kicked. The ball loomed skyward rolling end over end and I was hoping it was not coming to me. No such luck! The ball landed in my arms. I felt like Spartacus must have felt in the center of the coliseum just after the Romans released the lions!

Now that I had the ball, my spring training kicked in. I started running down the field trying to pick up my blockers. I would zig left, zag right. The run back was only about ten yards, but it seemed to take forever. Fear puts life in slow motion. My kick off return ended when I found myself flying in the air backwards in the opposite direction. I was heading back to the same spot that I had been when I caught the ball. I was tackled to the ground and quickly jumped up. I was not hurt. I felt great as I returned to the huddle. The roar and cheers of the crowd made me feel like a celebrity. I was drunk with fame. My fear was gone. I now plan on dating one of the cheerleaders…if I make a touchdown, I may even date the LEAD cheerleader. "I love football!"

Winter rolls in and basketball season starts. Shandon High was so small that almost every boy in the school played on one of the three teams. We had "A", "B", and "C" teams. Our games were played on Friday nights. Everyone in the jostling community attended these games with the utmost vigor. There were a total of five schools in our league. This included schools from Templeton, San Simeon, Morrow Bay, and Quiama. A rode trip to another school could take up to five hours driving time. We, the players and the citizens of the community, absolutely looked forward to the Friday games. We didn't always win, but that didn't make the crowd cheer less for us. What a thrill to have five hundred people screaming and yelling for you to make a score!

We played our home games in the gymnasium. We

48

had a wonderful gym with beautiful, shiny hardwood floors. When the games were over the crowd would leave and the high school kids would stay. This would allow us to hold a dance in the gymnasium. Someone would bring a record player and a cache of the top tunes. Pat Boone and Elvis seemed to be the top. Because we were dancing on the hardwood floors we were not allowed to wear any shoes. The dance was called a "sock-hop".

After reaching age sixteen, I no longer needed Alvis to drive me on my dates. I now have a driver's license that would allow me to date alone. This is what I always wanted to do!

The old fire-eating-dragon, called "the car", was needing restoration that would bring any damsel looking for a suitor to the high school dances. Because I was not a seamstress, nor was I an upholsterer, I was lucky enough to beg for the services of my wonderful mother who could sew or make anything. Mother had made apparel for many weddings. Everyone in the community wanted a wedding dress for their lovely daughters that would photograph as an American beauty that would last forever.

I did not need a wedding dress. What I needed was my money-eating-dragon restored. Mother was great because (I think) I was her favorite! Mother agreed to help me re-upholster the entire inside of my 1950 Chevrolet. She didn't know what "tuck and roll" meant, but I explained to her that that was what everyone else was putting into their cars. I stripped the car of all parts that fabric touched. Mother re-upholstered everything to my specifications.

Now I needed a paint job. Alvis had a girlfriend whose dad offered to paint my car for $5 dollars. This would cover the cost of the paint. I would sand and mask and he would "shoot". While the paint job was being done outside, I didn't mind the slight orange peel because I had chosen the vivid color of turquoise. After a month, my car looked so cool that given the opportunity, LaBamba would steal it if the doors were left unlocked!

While this car did not show a dancing Mexican girl on the dashboard, it did reveal a sparsely clad female on the Brody knob. The Brody knob was a clamp-on circle attached to the steering wheel. With this now illegal device on the steering wheel, when I pushed the throttle to the floor in a sharp turn the mud and dust would fly like I was in control of unlimited horsepower. This was a common event in 1962. The Brody knob allowed me to turn the wheel as fast as I could rotate one arm. This added to the beauty of the dice that were hanging from the rear view mirror.

I was luckier than most sixteen year olds that possessed a cool rod. My older brother, John, was a stud so I was the recipient of women's earrings glistening the visors on both sides of my car! The earrings represented how many gorgeous women had been in this car. While

these glistening earrings were never possessed by the
women I dated, it gave the appearance that I had dated
fifty foxes plus! This was like enjoying the experience of
having a ten-inch dick! When other unsuccessful would-
be-studs saw the prized earrings on my visors, they
thought I was the stud! I left that thought just as it was!!!

Being lucky enough to have a role model like John, I
always wanted to be just like him. Every time Alvis and
I would see John in town he would be caressing an eye
catching blonde-haired beauty with big boobs! Sweaters
were "in" then and I liked the sweaters! Alvis and I
figured that Big John was getting more ass than a toilet
seat! Later in life he denied this....I never believed a
word of his denial!

Once a year while staying with tradition, the school's
annual events would include the legendary hayride. The
hayride required cattle trucks laced with straw that
would drive to a secret destination. This destination
would journey to a roaring campfire on top of a remote
hill. At the fire we would all sit around, sing, laugh, and
have fun. No one went on a hayride unless they had a
date. My one and only hayride was a complete disaster.
After fearing rejection for a month I finally got the nerve
to ask a girl to attend with me. I was extremely careful
not to ask any beautiful girl that might be dating one of
the "big boys". Instead, I asked an average looking girl
that was also in my class. She said yes and the date was
set. I picked her up at 6:00 p.m. and we were off. I
couldn't help but notice the hundreds of freckles
covering here cute face. (Maybe I had a thing for

freckles!?!) She said that her mother had told her not to worry about them because they would all disappear by the time she was grown. I figured she would have to kiss a frog if there was any real hope of her mother's statement coming true!

Soon, the kids started arriving at the school parking lot to begin boarding the trucks. As darkness fell upon the school ground my date and I boarded the truck and we were off to the secret location. This was the time to smooch and cuddle. We couldn't have traveled more than one mile when I noticed dust and straw floating in the air. I just remembered that I could have an exaggerated acute reaction to straw and dust. This reaction is called "hay fever"! Not being able to wrap my head in wet towels, as I did when working in the fields of Bitterwater, I would just have to suffer. Having no opportunity to communicate with the driver, I knew the truck was not going to stop. I had no choice but to sit still and try to fight off the symptoms. The ride seemed like it took ten hours! Finally, the truck stopped. Everyone piled out and rushed to the roaring bonfire. My date and I approached the fire and I figured that I would recover the catastrophic embarrassment of mucus running from my nose. In the glowing light of the fire my date, showing extreme concern, looked at me and asked, "Are you all right?"

I replied, "I am fine. Why do you ask?"

She stated, "I notice that your eyes are swollen shut

and you have wet snot drooling down the front of your shirt!"

That was the last time she spoke to me for the rest of the night. After the long truck ride back to the school we quietly slid into the front seat of my car. I put my arm around her and told her I was sorry and I went for a kiss. She shunned the kiss and said that I was totally disgusting. She wouldn't kiss me.

I asked, "Since you won't kiss me, does this mean that a blow job is out of the question?"

That was the last hayride I ever went on and my last date with her!

By my senior year I was now on the Varsity teams. I was actually Team Captain and Quarterback of the football team. I was a star! For the last three years I had thrown many seventy-yard touch down passes. I was a seasoned pro. I was dating the lead cheerleader. One day the two hundred and seventy-five pound center on the football team and my good buddy suggested that, because we were seniors, we should all grow beards for the appearance of looking "tough". I said, "As Captain of this team, we will stay with the school tradition and maintain a clean cut appearance." I thought that growing a beard would be a neat thing, but I also knew that I was hormonally challenged and couldn't grow anything except peach fuzz! The team did not grow beards that year. To this day, I still cannot grow a full beard and the fuzz on my chest has turned to three, gray hairs! I should have been born of an Italian family!

To me, attending high school was like attending Harvard. There were seven teachers and we changed classrooms every hour. We also had a wonderful agriculture program for the FFA boys. Most of the boys elected to follow in their father's footsteps and pursue a career in farming, so FFA was where it was "at". Their classes were easy with little English or Mathematics required. I did not take any FFA classes because we had no ranch and my future plans did not include working for a rancher. Unfortunately, the only classes left for ME to take were Math, English, and Science.

While I wasn't in FFA, my brother Alvis was. He had two sheep and in the month of September all of the FFA boys from the entire county would attend the big event, The Annual County Fair. This was the opportunity for the high school boys to get to wear their corduroy blue jackets with gold embroidery boasting their school names. They wore those like they were going to West Point! The FFA boys would be excused for one week of classes. They would show off the beautiful animals that their dads' had reared! Alvis and all of the boys would stay at the fairgrounds twenty-four hours a day and sleep with their animals. I somehow finagled my way into going with Alvis to the county fair. I couldn't pass up this opportunity to fraternize with the girls, drink beer, and party all night!

I can honestly tell you that I never touched one of those sheep because we all know that sheep don't lie!!!

Today, people living in the big cities refer to country living as romantic and peaceful. I saw it as miles from fun and even further to romance.

Chapter 8

After dating for two years, I realized that the probability of ever having sex with a woman was slim without the promises of marriage. My approach to my new girlfriend was that I would pursue this relationship as a "prelude to marriage". This worked very well. However, after six months of wonderful sex I was rewarded with the news that I was going to be a father. This was NOT good news! I felt like I had been caught robbing a bank. The girl that was with child was sixteen years old. I was only seventeen! Her father was a rancher with many acres of land, a member of the school board, and owned a huge shotgun! Figuring that I would be dead by Monday, I swore to my dad that I was madly in love and wanted to get married...knowing that what I said was not what I wanted to do; I was also scared of what would happen if my other plan was executed.

Dad was very understanding. He said, "You made your bed...now sleep in it!" I did.

As wonderful and understanding as Dad was, I now realize that Dad grew up as a sharecropper in West Texas with ten other siblings. In the 1920's and 1930's sex was not allowed. Sex was taboo. Dad was a prude. (Mom was too!)

Now that I am married and feel like an adult I will

raise my family just like "Ward and June Cleaver". In February 1962 my son, Adam, was born. We were almost the same age. He was zero and I was eighteen! At this time I was working as a "Mr. Goodwrench" at a gas station in the small spot outside of Bitterwater called Cholame. This was the spot where James Dean was killed in his 1955 Porsche. The monument still stands.

Things were good. My wife's parents had provided us with a wonderful place to live on their big wheat and cattle ranch. It was just a plot of land near a small lookout tower called Annette Lookout. (This tower was built to watch for range fires and later, during WWII, was used to watch for air attacks from the Japanese. My new father-in-law had been assigned to the grueling task of manning this strategic location during the war.) Now that I had a nice piece of land to live on there was just one problem…there was no house on this piece of land. This was not a problem for long because good fortune was coming down the road. It was an enormous eight by forty foot trailer house headed to the spot that was designated for us to live!

After my excitement was contained my father-in-law, Ben Carpenter, handed me a payment book of coupons! I now owed HIS bank $8000 dollars to pay off the biggest debt of anyone's conception. This mobile fort, the new house trailer, was a surprise to me…as was the payment book!

At this point my life is good, but I think that I am no

longer in charge. I drive twenty miles to Cholame to pump gas for $1.63 per hour and then home. Now in my small life the world seems to be two hundred miles in diameter.

Now that I am married, the gas station job no longer suited me. Pumping gas was usually something reserved for pimple-faced kids. I am now an adult and I will take a job at the local grocery store. This new job proves to be no fun and pays less than I was earning at the gas station.

During those days, I recall a moment in history that changed my life forever. It was October 1962. I noticed that business was better than usual and everyone coming into the store was buying all of the food that their pocketbook could support. Soon, I learned that we were nearing the threat of a nuclear war with the black devil called Russia. The end of the world is coming! I went home and watched the news. President Kennedy had just given the Russians the doomsday ultimatum: "Remove the missiles from Cuba, or we will attack with nuclear weapons!" The war didn't happen and within three days all threats of war were forgotten; however, the world was frozen in fear for the remaining two weeks.

I never wanted to be poor nor did I want to be directed by anyone. One morning I decided to look for a job that paid more and would allow me to move away. In those days, freedom meant moving one hundred miles from Mother, Dad, and In-Laws.

I had decided that being married did not necessarily prove to our parents that we were adults. In order to get along with my new in-laws, I had to allow them to treat me without respect. After one year of kissing up to Ben C. and allowing him to make my choices, I was blessed by fate with the job offer of the century…a job working for the same oil company as my dad. This meant good money and moving to Taft…one hundred miles away…ureka!

My first day on the job was great. I was given the opportunity to change tires on the huge trucks. I was assigned to work with an older man. He said he was twenty years old and if I wanted to succeed in my new job I must do as he said!

Three weeks later I could not believe my eyes…my check was two times what it was when I worked in the gas station! I was now making $3.00 per hour. The year is 1963. Things are great! Two promotions later, I am now making $3.75 an hour. This is the same amount of money that Dad was making.

Now that I have this newborn wealth, I realize that I can afford a new car. Monday after work I proudly walk into my bank to apply for a loan to purchase a brand new 1964 Ford Falcon. The car cost $2400 dollars. The bank loan manager told me that they do not make loans for cars to boys nineteen years of age. I went home feeling like I had been kicked in the groin. My desire to own that car occupied my thoughts twenty-four seven.

On Tuesday the following week I went back to the bank and wanted a recount. The Grinche's manager said that he would grant the loan if I could acquire a bona fide co-signer.

With this new information in hand I hustled back to the Bitterwater pump station. Mother, Dad and Little Sister were still there. After explaining to Dad what a great car I have decided to buy, I was given the crunching disappointment of Dad telling me "no" to co-signing.

For a nineteen year old, this is not an option. After loving Mom and Dad good-bye my wife and I drove twenty miles north to the Ben C. Ranch. I gave the sob story of Dad telling me "no" to my father-in-law. The story worked. Ben signed the paper for the bank loan. I said "Thanks Dad!"

We drove one hundred miles back to Taft and the bank seemed like two thousand miles. The loan was approved and I had my car.

My job was going good, but driving a truck in a remote area with nothing but oil wells all around…things started getting boring. Also, my marriage has been strained as we have lost our second born to SIDS. Life goes on.

At work one day I hear the news that JFK had been assassinated. I didn't know much about JFK.

When I was in high school "vacation" to me meant school is out so get a job. Because of my wonderful job with the oil company, it meant go away for two weeks. "Where will I go?"

During my last few years of living at home with my parents I had observed the travels of my older sister and brother moving onto bigger and better places. My oldest sister, Pukette, had remarried a flamboyant salesman that had brought to the family excitement and new ideas that no one had ever heard. Henry was the best-dressed man that God had ever put on this green earth. It didn't take me long to know that I wanted to be just like him. He WAS Harold Hill, the Music Man!

Henry, while being flamboyant, was also a man that offered dreams for the future. Not unlike a trip to a place where the evils are controlled, the speed is fast, the colors are vivid, and the slow are left behind. Pukette and Henry now live in Seattle. To me, that sounds like the moon!

I have the greatest job in the world at the oil pipeline plant in Taft. I am happy. My wife loves me and my son is perfect!

Now back to vacation. "Why don't we go to Seattle this year on our vacation?"

This idea changed my whole life. Like jumping through a black hole. "OK gang, jump in the car and let's drive to Seattle and visit Aunt Pukette and Uncle Henry!"

We arrived in Seattle. What a place! Seattle was big. Even bigger than big! I had never seen anything like this in my life. There were beautiful mountains, water everywhere, huge evergreen trees, and big buildings. The homes looked like the ones I saw on TV and in movies. Now I have been to Shandon and Bakersfield, but I have never seen anything like Seattle.

Seattle was like a brass band blasting down the street of Paso Robles on Pioneer Day. Everyone looked rich! I believed that if I could move to Seattle I would be rich too! Six months was all it'd take! Kind of sounds like the "Gold Rush"! After discovering the "mother load", I decided we should move to Seattle.

On the return trip to Taft and back to "Uncle Toms Cabin" my lovely wife and I discussed moving to Seattle. I don't really remember if she wanted to move or not.

In June 1965, my family and I excitedly moved to heaven...Seattle!!! We rented a house in Ballard. This is a community of Norwegians and Swedes. It only took me one week to realize that these people had never heard of Bitterwater. The house we lived in was old, but it was the most beautiful and comfortable house I had ever seen. The rent was $100 dollars per month.

Life is looking good. We now have a daughter. Her name is Jenny.

My first job was selling cars. My God! I am a failure! To sell cars you must have the "best deal". I didn't think this was possible. Lots of people are selling cars. How is it possible for me to sell a car cheaper than anyone else? So much for my sales career!

I still live in a nice house. I need a job. After realizing I am not a salesman I start looking in the newspaper for employment. Gee wiz…there is a job at a commercial airplane company. This job requires that you possess the ability to read blueprints and understand the proper use of shop equipment. I have had twenty hours of training in blueprint reading at Shandon High School!!!!!!

Chapter 9

In June of 1965, I went to apply for the aircraft job.
The Human Resources' lady asked me, "What is your
name and social security number?"

I asked, "Why do you want to know my social security
number?"

She responded, "We want to know if you are a
convicted felon!"

I replied, "I don't even KNOW any convicted
felons!!!!"

Once the HR lady and I completed the statistics, she
sent me into another room to meet with a man named
Joe. He was going to interview me. He asked, "What's
your name? When were you born? When can you
start?"

I answered his questions as quickly as he asked them.
He then handed me an application and told me to
complete the form and then go into another room. He
advised me that there was a test in the other room and
once I completed this test, I should return to the HR lady.

I completed the application and the aptitude test that was waiting for me and returned to the HR lady. She didn't even look up, or review the test or application but simply stated, "We're offering you an entry level job. If you accept, we want you to report to work Monday!"

I accepted the offer.

Monday I was off to a good start. I didn't oversleep. With no time to shower, I brushed my teeth, combed by hair and headed for the door. Like Joe Namath, my wife faded back and threw the ball. The pass was complete. I caught my bologna sandwich! Ten minutes later I arrived at the aircraft plant and quickly found a parking space. I jumped out of the car and briskly walked toward the security guard shack. After displaying my Company Identification Badge, I was given the nod to proceed onto Company property. I walked about one half a mile when I finally entered the huge building that would be my workplace for the next year.

Inside the building I could see industrial machines everywhere. Rows and rows of these machines were all around. This place was as clean as my sister, Pukette's, house. The floors were concrete and shined with the reflection of a still pond. As I glanced upward, my eyes were temporarily blinded by the brightness of the thousands of mercury lights hanging from the ceiling. They had created artificial sunlight. "WOW!" There was so much light that one could not even see their own shadow on the floor. Reminding me of my school days

65

past, I heard a piercing sound. It was the bell summoning us to start the shift. Everyone in the shop promptly headed to their assigned work stations. All that was left were the twenty-three lost and confused new hires. I didn't have a clue what my duties would be, so I just stood there along with the others. I was so overwhelmed that I must have looked like a startled deer in the headlights of an oncoming car! While trying to make light of the situation, I looked over at a man standing next to me. I said to him, "I don't think we're in Kansas anymore Toto!" He didn't laugh, or even smile. I figured he must be Japanese!

Soon I was introduced to an elderly man. His name was Mike. He walked with a limp and needed a shave. He kind of reminded me of my Uncle Wilbur from Texas. He will be my boss for the next thirty days. Mike was very kind to me. He said, "I see we have twenty-three new hires here today. In order to assign you to your new job I must know your background. How far did you go in school?"

Eight said college grads, ten said Associates, and five said High School. It only took five minutes and Mike handed me a mop and a broom!

From 6:00 a.m. until 2:30 p.m. I would sweep and mop the concrete floors. Thirty days had elapsed and I was now a professional janitor. I was becoming proud of my beautiful floors and I didn't want anyone screwing them up. I now could cruise down the aisles with the grace and rhythm of an Olympic speed skater. As I started to round a corner leading to the homestretch, I was startled to a halt. A huge man resembling the "Incredible Hulk" stood before me. He was the ruling union member of the entire shop (shop steward). With a scowl on his face he handed me a piece of paper. I grabbed the paper and started to read: "Dear Mr. Johnson: Effective immediately, your employment with this Company is terminated!" "WOW! I just got fired!" After catching my breath, the steward explained to me that when I hired in I either would join the union, or write a letter to the union stating that I declined my membership. No one told me about that requirement. After careful negotiations, my termination was rescinded and from that day forward I would be paying union dues. "I love organized labor!"

My membership in the union was a bittersweet relationship. On one hand, the union negotiated benefits, good pay, free medical insurance, sick leave, and paid vacations. Dad was always an advocate for the unions. On the other hand, all too often, hard work was rarely rewarded. Seniority determined job preferences and career longevity. "Slow down, you will make me look bad!" That was the word of the "brotherhood"! I had low, or no seniority so with my one month of working the day shift, good things would come to an end. The boss informed me that the following Monday I would report to night shift (graveyard)! ' "Where's "Lurch"?'

The shift started at 11:30 p.m. and ended at 6:00 a.m. To me, this sounded like a pretty good deal. Six hours of work for eight hours of pay. I figured that I would be able to stay home, fish, and play during the day. Everyday will seem just like a day off! The first two days went very well. I was playing all day around the house and fishing in the salt waters of Puget Sound. By the third day I found myself having difficulty at keeping my eyes open and performing my duties at work. I could almost sleep standing on my feet. I got so sleepy that my boss told me to go home. The next night I reported for work and my boss explained to me, "Either learn how to sleep during the day, or find another job!" I worked night shift for the next four years!!!

Transitioning to graveyard shift had now become manageable. I had been promoted to the title of "toolmaker". After two years I had mastered the skill of reading airplane blueprints and I had become a darn good toolmaker. I got along well with most of the other employees and I felt that my boss and I had become good friends. One day for a few select employees a non-scheduled crew meeting was held. We were given instructions to report to a new plant in Everett…a fifty mile one–way drive from home! This meant I would spend three hours per day just for the commute. Driving to the plant in Everett soon became a bigger task than making tools. "Invention comes from necessity." (Thomas Edison.)

After a short search my wife and I rented a modest farmhouse, north of Everett, near Stanwood. This house had a huge red barn, a chicken coop, and sat on thirty-five acres. Now the drive to work would be thirty miles to the south! Not much of an improvement!

Now in the new plant, I was assigned to a crew that would build the wings for the world's largest airplane. Everyday we would measure and draw lines from sketches that would allow us to saw and file the shapes of the thick aluminum wing skins. The schedule was tight and a five-day workweek was no longer possible. I would work ten hours a day, seven days a week for the next six months. Forget any days off!

I had now been promoted to "crew leader". My crew was staffed with myself and ten other employees. I am twenty-two years old and have men in their fifties reporting to me! I will be a good boss! It didn't take long before I started noticing that the crew seemed to be getting smaller. I would walk around to see if I could account for all of them. I came to the realization that I could never see the entire crew at the same time. After a few days of "hide and seek", I finally figured out the problem. As their new boss, the men had no fear or respect for me. This pissed me off! I had to deal with the problem. The honeymoon was now over! I called the group to an area and explained that because I was in charge and I had now taken on the responsibility of production, we will work with the same enthusiasm as we all had done in the past. Some groaned and some even laughed! I was becoming even more pissed off! As I thought about what to do, I remembered one of my old bosses in Renton. He told me that if I could not learn to sleep during the day, I should find another job. I figured the strategy worked on me so maybe it will work FOR me. I took a deep breath, tucked in my shirt, and lowered my voice. "If you men can't return eight hours of work for eight hours of pay, I suggest that you start looking for another job!" Dead silence ensued. Without a word from anyone, the crew quickly returned to their current assignments. The game was now over and that was the end of our playing "hide and seek". I figured that by now everyone hated me and I was the talk of the lunchroom. To my surprise, I ended up with a very hard working, dedicated crew. I think they like me now. I learned that a boss must be not unlike that of a parent. He/she must counsel, console, protect, and direct. I am a good boss!

From 1967 thru 1969 we, by hand, built twenty-one sets of wings for the giant bird. My crew and I won many awards. This included coffee mugs, hats, and pictures! Life was good and I was finally starting to feel like an adult. This prolific lifestyle would go on forever. At this time we were in the Nixon era and we just couldn't wait for wage control. What is wage control? That is when you can almost pay your bills if you don't get the raise you were promised last year!

Chapter 10

During those youthful years I always pursued my passions to hunt and fish. I had purchased a boat and enjoyed many weekends fishing on the vast confines of Puget Sound. In the late 60's, the fishing for salmon and cod was world class. I always took my oldest son, Adam. With him I never felt alone. Being twenty-two years of age and fishing with my four year old son was more fun than being poked in the eye with a sharp stick. I will never forget those precious days.

Now that I have become a seasoned "Washingtonian" a vacation to me meant traveling south to my old stomping grounds of Bitterwater. October would find my family and I cruising down the I-5 corridor. I would always drive non-stop from Seattle to Bitterwater. This would take eighteen butt-flattening hours! I chose October as the month for our vacation because that would be the start of the California deer-hunting season. This had become the biggest annual event for the male gender of the Johnson Family!

My family and I arrived in Bitterwater...home at last! We would greet Mother and Dad and start the usual self-guided tour of the old home digs. Each subsequent trip reveals the changes of time. The kitchen table has been replaced and Mother now has a dishwasher. The rug in the living & dining room is new. Dad's old overstuffed chair has been replaced with a new electric, heated, vibrating recliner. I would look around and notice that the rooms seemed to be much smaller than I had remembered as a child.

By now, my brothers and their families have arrived and we are all together...just like the old days. Mother is busy cooking her best meal from memories of the past. This meal will be her best recollection as to what our favorites were when we were all young. Mom was always a great cook. Dad was so glad to see us that he had not a clue as to what was the source of the succulent aroma teaming from the kitchen. I was always so happy to be back in Bitterwater with Mother and Dad. Mother could have been cooking bologna and sauerkraut...I wouldn't have cared.

Dinner is ready and Mother has now summoned everyone to the table. She has prepared pot roast, homemade pinto beans, mashed potatoes & gravy. The dinner looked so good that everyone was salivating like one of Pavlov's dogs. We all enjoyed Mom's wonderful dinner. Later we will all have a choice of which homemade pie that she remembered was each and everyone's own favorite. My favorite was lemon cream.

After dinner and feeling stuffed like a Christmas goose, Dad and the boys retired to the living room. This was the time for Dad to explain what he had accomplished in preparation for the ensuing pack trip. The planning of the pack trip was always as exciting as the moment the pack train and we actually started up the trail. For the trip, in order to travel to the elevation of nine thousand feet to our base camp nestled in the high Sierra Mountains, we would need ample provisions to sustain us for ten days. The remote campsite was one that we had constructed many years earlier. No one else knew of, or could find this hidden place.

We would now plan all of the necessary food, camping gear, and the transportation. Our transportation to the high country would require the services of five strong horses. The horses we would ride would be Dad's three from Bitterwater and two of my older brother John's from Bakersfield. Dad's horses were now entering their golden years. One of Dad's horses was "Babe", a notorious maverick that was charged with the blood of a thoroughbred. Babe could run fifty miles per hour. She was not my idea of a packhorse, nor did I want to put my life in her hooves during any attempt to navigate the dangerous steep trail. The second horse was a Morgan named "Collect Call" that Dad had trained from a colt. He was as gentle as a lamb. The only problem with him was that he had an insurmountable fear of loud diesel trucks. If you were unfortunate enough to be riding Collect, you would feel like a lumbering cowboy until he detected the presence of an approaching truck. At this time he would become the star of the rodeo. He wouldn't stop bucking until he was pooped, or the rider was found picking his ass up off the ground!

My favorite horse since childhood was the old reliable mare we called "Sugar". She was white with a few black spots. Old Sugar was gentle and wouldn't hurt a fly.

However, this year Sugar would not be on the pack trip. She had become ill and had gone to horsy heaven the summer prior. Fortunately, two years before Sugar died she had dropped a beautiful, raspberry colored foal. Her foal was called "Missy". Missy had never been ridden before, but Dad had figured that she would learn the routine on the trail. The two horses that John was providing included a $15 dollar donkey. The horse's names were "Ginger" and "Big Red". The jackasses' name was "Dusty". Dusty and I will later become trail mates!

The day before deer season opened we loaded the animals, food, and gear in the trucks. By nightfall we had reached our first night's destination, the cabin. The women and children would stay warm and cozy there while the men hit the mountain trail out the following day.

The morning sunlight is breaking through the clouds just above the peak of Slate Mountain. With breakfast completed we reload the animals and head to the trailhead. At the bottom of the trailhead, the decision is being made as to who will ride what. With six animals, two would be packed and four would be ridden. John would ride his horse, Ginger; Alvis would ride John's other horse, Big Red; Dad would ride Babe because no one else would; and we would pack Collect and Missy. All that was left for me to ride was the jackass...Dusty! With the animals saddled and the packs tightly bound with the famous controversial diamond hitch we were off to conquer the trail. We looked like John Wayne headed up to the line shack on the winter range.

The trail was steep in spots and could be extremely dangerous. We were now a finely tuned pack train. Dusty and I are the "caboose". The horses were doing well, the sky was clear, and the view was even more spectacular than I had remembered from years past. We had now completed the easy parts of the winding, dusty trail. We would stop only momentarily to let the horses "blow". (Always let your horse blow, but never blow your horse!) The little pack train was now at the halfway point to camp. Things were going just too good. All of the sudden all hell broke loose. The rodeo was on! The announcer would have said, "Out of the number one shoot comes three time world champion bronco rider, Alvis Johnson, riding Big Red!" Everything would have been fine were it not that Alvis was also leading Collect, one of the packhorses. Everywhere that Big Red went Collect would follow.

John loudly yelled, "Alvis, let go of the lead rope!"

Alvis yelled back, "I'm not holding the rope!"

Up, down, over the bushes they went. If this had been a real rodeo, Alvis would have been disqualified. He was gripping the saddle horn so hard that he must have left fingerprints.

Suddenly, as quickly as the rodeo had started, Big Red stopped in his tracks. We figured that the event was over.

The problem that influenced the horse to buck was a result of the lead rope from the packhorse had somehow become entangled under the tail of Big Red. I will save the day! I jumped off of my trusty jackass and proceeded to the rear end of the flustered horse. Now I could easily see that Big Red had clamped down on the rope with his mighty tail. He had clamped that rope with a force similar to the "jaws of life"! With a huge jerk, I yanked that bound rope attempting to remove it from under the tail. Big Red must have liked that rope under his tail because as soon as the rope was free the rodeo was on again. Up, down, up, down! As quickly as it had started the rodeo was over and all was back to business as usual. I was glad that Alvis was the world champ instead of me! "I will stay with my jackass!"

By now the sun was slowly disappearing behind the distant snow capped peaks. Camp was just around the next bend. Good news! No one else had found or was occupying our campsite. Camp included two rock formed fire pits with a huge log nearby. Next to camp was a clear mountain, artesian spring gushing from the ground. This spring was adjacent to a beautiful, lush green meadow of approximately three acres. The horses will be well watered and fed.

Soon we had the camp put in order and the livestock

had been put up for the night. Dad would hobble and tie only the lead horse. We hoped the others would not leave. Babe was, no doubt, the leader. Just like wild Mustangs without ropes or any saddles, these horses blended with the surroundings of nature.

Winter comes early in the high country. The aspen trees were already showing the red and yellow colors of fall. It would still be warm during the daylight hours, but at night frost was the rule. With cool nights, our groceries would be well preserved. The sleeping bags were rolled out and we would all lie in our beds next to the campfire and gaze up at the glistening stars. The air was so clear at nine thousand feet that the view was totally unobstructed. We could even see satellites pass overhead on their high-speed journey through space.

We were awakened to the old familiar call we had heard many times before from the old man, "Up and at 'em! Drop your cocks and grab your socks!" Dad learned that quote in the Navy. Not wanting to embrace the cold morning air, my brothers and I would reluctantly crawl out of our sleeping bags. Dad already had the fire blazing and the coffee hot. That was the only cooking Dad would do for the entire trip! I think that Dad thought that knowing how to cook would make him a sissy. Sissy, or not…I'm hungry! John and I did most of the cooking; however, Alvis liked burning the bacon and floating the eggs! As we ate our burned bacon and floating eggs, we were all anxious to hit the woods.

Everyone thought that this year would be the year that they would take their trophy of a lifetime. Alvis and John took off on foot, as usual, heading for their favorite spot. This was where success had embraced them years past. I stayed with dad and we would head to another location. The area we hunted was no larger than one square mile. We were on a plateau, a flat bench surrounded by vertical cliffs. These cliffs would oversee many steep rockslides. Some of these slides would cover the slope thousands of feet to the bottom of the canyons. Dad and I enjoyed our morning hunt, but saw no game. Upon returning to camp we noticed that John and Alvis were still gone. It was about 1 o'clock in the afternoon when they shuffled into camp. They stated that they hadn't seen anything and that we should prepare lunch. Lunch usually consisted of a can of beans and a giant bologna sandwich!

The morning hunts were never as successful as the evening hunts because in the evening the deer were usually on a specific route to a water hole. The water hole was the same spot that Alvis and John had visited that morning. After grabbing a small nap, the "mountain men" would start their evening pursuit. John and Alvis had decided to return to their favorite spot near the brushy water hole. The water hole was at the head of an almost vertical cliff and any deer in there would be very difficult to see in the thick brush and rock cover. John, while sitting high in the rocks above the water hole, was trying to clear his eyes from the cold, whistling wind blowing up the vertical canyon. As he wiped his eyes, he noticed the arrival of two, huge majestic bucks. He waved the signal to Alvis and Alvis was quickly on the scout. John and Alvis , simultaneously, would raise their trusty rifles and fire! The shots were so close together that neither could hear the other one shoot. Alvis's deer dropped like a rock and will become "meat in the freezer". John's deer, however, didn't flinch. He took off running and John had figured he had missed. Quickly chambering another round, he fired again. The deer dropped. Both would be hunters had filled their tags and their hunt was over. Alvis had slowly approached the deer he had taken and started the task of field dressing. John headed for the spot he had last seen his deer. He found his deer, but noticed there was one problem...it had no antlers! Does were not legal and bucks must display horns showing two points or better on at least one side or the other. At this time he believed that his eyes had betrayed him. He could not accept the mistake that he had made, but fortune was soon to come. As he looked at the head of the carcass he noticed two round circles between the ears. He had done something that no one had ever heard of. He had literally shot the antlers off of his buck's head! Now happy to know that he was not seeing things he still didn't have a buck with antlers. Alvis and John searched the brush for about an hour and were able to find just one of the missing antlers. Even though the antler was not attached to the deer, John, being a Deputy Sheriff, believed that he could convince any Game Warden that he had taken a legal deer. Dusk was now setting in and it was not possible for them to drag these deer the long distance back to camp before total darkness would set in. They decided to leave their deer where they lay until the following morning.

John and Alvis returned to camp and shared the story of their successful hunt. Tonight we will have a celebration. "Break out the corn whisky!" We loved to sit around the campfire and talk about those moments for years to come.

The next morning we saddled up two horses and headed for the spring where the deer had been left the previous night. Hoping that a bear had not disturbed our bounty we were relieved to see that everything was in tact. Now we had a problem. The deer were approximately two hundred yards down the steep canyon and we would not be able to get the horses down there to pack them out. We three boys climbed down the cliff and began dragging Alvis's deer up the hill one step at a time. Two hours later, the deer was on high ground and could be loaded onto Big Red. We now had to return down the slope to get the other deer and repeat the same grueling pack up the cliff. We didn't get half way up the hill when Dad yelled out, "That's far enough. I'll bring the horse down and pick it up!"

We could not believe what we were hearing. That cliff was so steep that we could barely stand. Dad led the horse down to where we were standing and we began loading the deer on the horse. Dad did not lead the horse up the hill because he did not want the horse stepping on him. Like an old Texas cowboy, he joined the deer in the saddle and he was off! The horse would take one step forward and slide two steps back. We were so concerned that dad, the deer, and the horse would fall down that canyon and roll out of site. Dad, on the horse, continued making slow progress up the hill. Soon Collect had decided that the task of walking up that hill wasn't possible so without notice he kneeled down and proceeded to crawl up the incline on his belly. The progress was slow, but Dad, the horse, and deer actually reached the top before we did.

We continued the hunt for a few more days, but any more success was not to be ours. I didn't get my deer that year, but the memory of that old-fashioned pack trip will be burned in my memory forever.

Chapter 11

Working at the aircraft company was wonderful. But, after four years of work, I was told by a Company spokesperson that they would no longer require my services. The money was gone by Friday. I had never been laid off before in my life.

After getting my lay-off notice telling me that that day would be my last day to build the airplanes of the future, I slowly walked out to the parking lot for another marathon of fighting two hours of traffic just trying to access the public street. The men I worked with suggested that we stop at the local pub and celebrate our new found freedom. After four years of building airplanes, surprisingly, I felt happy to be laid off. I believed that the Company had just lost someone that it will not survive without. The truth was that the Company was so large that to lose me was like losing a drop in a bucket. Monday morning, I was missing it.

With that…within two months my marriage of five years had ended. "Free at last!" (Martin Luther King.)

Now I am alone. I have no money! I have no family! I have no job! I have only me!!! When the judge got through with me, I realized that there was no justification for any man to ever get divorced and I should be punished. The wrath hit me hard! I lost everything: the children, all family possessions, and a wife that I had believed loved me. But the good news is that I got all of the bills and I will get to pay child support until the children reach majority. This means that I will be "Uncle Dad" for the rest of my life!

Well, now I find myself twenty-four years old, broke, single, and living in Seattle – the most beautiful place in the world.

At this time in most people's lives, they may consider giving up. I didn't realize how much fun it was to be out of work until the bills started coming in. Soon the phone started ringing and I had completely run out of excuses as to why I could not pay my creditors. My time now is being occupied pounding the pavement seeking a new job. Things are tough in beautiful Seattle. One hundred thousand people were laid off in a period of just four months. Times were so hard that even engineers were begging for a job at Mickey-D's. I was not qualified to work there! Thinking back to my childhood in Bitterwater I would recall the proud words of my father. He would boast that he had never collected any unemployment or welfare in his entire poverty stricken life. I could not hold out any longer.

To maintain my life support systems, I knew that I must have food and shelter. The state will assist me with $40 dollars per week unemployment for a period of thirteen weeks. This money was great! It was enough to pay one half of my bills and child support. I looked for work everywhere. There were just no jobs to be found. Sounds like "The Big Depression" of the 30's. Dad and Mother lived through "The Big Depression" and they knew that what I was going through was not as bad as what they had suffered. I felt better just knowing that! In those days, a Swanson TV Dinner cost .35 cents and a bologna sandwich was a dime. I ate one or the other everyday! Being like my dad with great resolve, I continued looking for a job!

I only wish that I looked as good today as I did then...I was lean, thin and gorgeous!

Although I was collecting unemployment, I never stopped looking for a job. One day, to my surprise, an acquaintance of mine told me that she was a bartender at Sandpoint Naval Station in Seattle and that her boss was looking for an experienced bartender to work nights. I said that I was his man. I started working Monday as a bartender. I, in those days, was not much of a drinker so I didn't know one drink from another.

On my first day, I was ready to poor a beer from the tap. I remember my first customer. His name was Sergeant Mad Dog. He said that he wanted twelve whiskey sours.

I stated, "I do not know how to make a whiskey sour and why do you want twelve of them?"

He responded, "Put one shot of whiskey and one shot of lemon juice in a glass with ice. The reason I want twelve is because I do not want to wait in line to get another drink."

I replied, "Sounds right to me!"

The bar I worked in was called The EMC (The Enlisted Men's Club). The patrons didn't want to be in the military so they had an attitude like "if you give me any shit I will kick your ass!" Some of these recruits returned from the war with emotional scars that not even a bartender could deal with. I heard stories of death and deception. Many were waiting for court marshal, but they still spent their free time in my bar. The bar was huge and I was the only bartender in the entire building and the only civilian. The year was 1970...Vietnam coming home! As the troops were returning home, I was always reminded that I didn't serve and I should be shot dead! Not to forget that the bar down the road was the "4, 5, 6 Club", or better known as the "Officer's Club". At the time that I accepted the job at The EMC bar I was unaware that two bartenders had been shot dead by a confused returning Veteran at this bar down the road.

After six months of pouring bar and learning how to make a Singapore Sling, I was beginning to be accepted as one of them. I was now third base player on their softball team.

One night while I was closing I had a small problem with one of the Shore Patrol guys. His name was Sergeant Akin. The Sergeant was with a young female that looked twenty-one MINUS! I politely told the Serg that I have to close...the time was 2:00 a.m. Serg was a big man. He taught hand-to-hand combat and martial arts to a Special Forces group. His specialty was to kill in two seconds. As I suggested to the Serg that he should leave, he said that he wanted another round. I decided that this request would not be possible. I don't think he was happy with this information.

He grabbed me by my arm and demanded, "Give us another drink or you will be crawling out on you knees!'

After a short thought of what that would be like, I decided that I was not man enough to whip his ass. I thought, "What should I do to stay alive?"

After another short moment of thought, I looked at the killer Serg and said that I have friends that love to fight and if he would let me go I would call them and they would come over and he could kick THEIR ass!

He said, "Go get them!"

After he released me from his humbling grip, I went to the phone and called his co-workers. We call them the "S.P.s'!"

I told the S.P.s' that Serg wanted to kick their asses!

They said, "Fine!"

Two minutes later, two S.P.s' showed up! I felt like WE could now kick his ass!

I told the Serg that these are my friends and I wanted him to leave the bar. Even though he worked with the S.P.s', he stood up and said that he would kick their ass too!

The S.P. on my left hit the Serg with a baton right between the eyes. He went down like a rock! Soon, he was handcuffed and held away. I felt tough!

Well tomorrow is another day and I knew that the Serg would be out of the brig! It was only a matter of time when he would come back to the bar and kill me. While at work the next night I saw this huge figure coming down the steps and heading straight for me! I felt like an Iraqi standing in the desert with a smart bomb looking for me!

As the Serg moved closer, I reached below the bar and slowly grabbed a huge wrench used to change the valves on the beer tank. I am ready!!!!!!

When the Serg got close I asked, "What can I do for you?"

With tears in his eyes he said that he was sorry and that he did not want me to serve him any more Singapore Slings.

I slowly and quietly returned the wrench to under the bar and replied, "OK." I fed the Serg cokes on the house the rest of the night!

Later in the night while I was busy serving the endless line of thirsty drinkers, a young sailor of about twenty-one ordered a pitcher of beer and two glasses. I served him as I did everyone and the night continued. I later noticed that the young sailor was sitting in the far back corner of the bar in a dark area. I also observed that he was not alone. He was with a very young lady that looked to be about sixteen years old. This pissed me off! I went to the back of the bar. I said nothing as I grabbed the pitcher of beer and I also grabbed the glass the young lady was holding. As I headed back to the bar I felt wind passing by my right ear. As I ducked, a glass of beer hit the mirror and glass went everywhere. I looked back and the young sailor was running for the door. I also observed the big, bad Sergeant Akin running behind the young sailor. Well, they were gone. Five minutes later the Serg returned from the stairway. I noticed that he had blood on his shirt. It was obvious to me that he had severely beaten the young sailor. He grimly looked over to me and said, "No one throws a glass at my friend!"

I never went to Vietnam, but a little bit of Vietnam had come to me. I quit my job that night!

My next job was even more fun than picking shit with the chickens! I was now working for the Seattle Skid Road Community Council. My job was to assist street people in discovering a place to eat and sleep. While these places were not hidden from them, they were hidden from public view. We never gave them cash, but we gave them meal tickets. These tickets were good for one meal at some of the low-end restaurants.

Before working on the street I always thought that collecting unemployment and welfare was something that worthless and lazy people do. After spending time with these homeless people, I started to realize that the reason that they were there was because they were incapable of putting together a bona fide plan that would include prioritizing daily activities. That would include reporting to a job and managing the money that resulted from that activity. I now know that these people needed help. My politics have been affected ever since!

As I became reliable at reporting to court every Monday morning, I wonder if life could ever offer more. I was in court on Mondays because that is when all of the street people that got arrested for vagrancy and drunkenness over the weekend were arraigned. My job was to speak for them and convince the judge that I had a house for them and they would not be on the street anymore. I'd sit there thinking that I cannot save the world. I must save me!

Chapter 12

I have met a wonderful lady and I am now married…again! "Ward and June Cleaver" are back! My new wife is working at a large department store downtown Seattle on Fifth Avenue. Life is good again!

However, the economy in beautiful Seattle is still in the dumps. One day I got the brilliant idea that somewhere in this great country there must be the "right" job for me! This was a time when there was no internet. The only way of reading a newspaper from another city was to drive to that city or go to the local library. The last time I had been to a library was my second year of high school. I found the local library in the big city. There were newspapers from everywhere. After hours of searching the help wanted ads, I came to the hopeful conclusion that the big job was in Denver, Colorado!

Hallelujah! Income tax refund! You have passed "go"…collect $300 dollars! My new wife and I are on our way to Denver! At that time I was the proud owner of a 1959 VW Beetle. My wife, Anne, drove a 1962 AMC Rambler. Her car was better than mine. "Let's sell my Bug, buy a trailer, and hit the road to new digs." ("There's gold in them there hills!")

We slept in the car along side the road. A huge nap lasted just two hours.

After fourteen hundred anxious miles, we arrived in a city that was as big as Seattle. Lights everywhere. On our first night we stayed at the Holiday Inn. Too much money, but I felt lucky!

The next morning I made calls to companies that sounded like they made products similar to the things that I had made at the airplane company. I landed a job on my first day in Denver. I was now a "Methods Analyst". This was a good job. While opening a bank account at the local bank, I asked if they needed any new employees. They said, "Yes"! I went home and told Anne the story and she was working there the next day. Life is good!

Denver in the 70's was still a growing city. Many people from East and West wanted to ski in Aspen and Vail. "Rocky Mountain High!" (John Denver.)

My new job was going well. I met a co-worker. His name was Dennis Roberts. He became a very nice and humble friend. Dennis was the proud father of three. Being a traditional Catholic family, his wife did not work. While money was not tight for us, it was to them. Dennis wanted to supplement his income. One day he asked me, "Why don't you and I take on the easy task of selling firewood to the people that have bought new homes with fireplaces?"

At the age of twenty-six, cutting firewood seemed like

something that would be like a walk in the park. After acquiring a wood permit from the Forest Service we couldn't wait to start our new business. Many people do not realize that Denver is one hundred miles from any place that trees grow. We would drive one hundred miles west to the spot where wood was available. I was used to the trees in the state of Washington. They are smooth with few knots, easy to cut, and split. In Colorado, the trees are true knotty pines. This meant tough to cut and harder to split. Dennis and I spent four months every Saturday and Sunday cutting and splitting knotty pine. Selling the wood was easy. We sold sixty chords that summer. We got $60 dollars per chord. After figuring out the balance sheet, we were proud to boast a huge profit of $2.00 per hour. I thought that this is not very good! That was the end of my wood cutting business!

Life is now too good for anyone to be satisfied and I knew it was time to screw it up!

Being the dreamer I have always been, I often thought of gold and living in the wilderness. One day while at work I thought it would be a novel idea to move to the rugged and wild frontiers of Alaska. My wife, Anne, was also ready for a change. We quit our secure jobs, sold our furniture, and loaded our car and pickup truck. The next day we were off to the Klondike. We drove to Seattle and booked passage on a steamer to the mythical state of Alaska.

Our plan was to homestead. Alaska, in 1971, was the only state in the Union that still offered land to would be homesteaders. The path to Alaska would require a ride on a ferryboat. While starting from Seattle, the ferry would travel north through the inside passage and onto Skagway. My wife and I had little money so we slept on the deck of the ferry for three nights. I felt like a 49'er. Once we arrived at Skagway we set out on the Alaskan Highway to Anchorage. This drive was longer and rougher than anyone could have imagined. It was one thousand miles of dirt road. Gas stations were one hundred miles apart. I loved it! The first day I wanted to drive until dark. This was not possible because in July, it NEVER GETS DARK!

Third stop was Toke Junction. The road sign read, "Turn right to Fairbanks. Turn left to Anchorage." We went left. Anchorage was much bigger than I had dreamed. The population of Anchorage was one hundred thousand.

Wanting to manage what little money we had wisely, I started looking for a bargain motel. "Wow!" The cheapest motel was twice as expensive as the Holiday Inn was in Denver. I took the room! After three nights of sleeping on a boat deck and in the cold, I wanted a REAL bed!

The next day I bought a newspaper to cruise the help wanted ads. There was a job listed for an experienced aircraft mechanic. I thought that I was a good aircraft mechanic. This job required the ability to refurbish Piper Super Cubs for short field and take-off landings. We called it STOL. I showed up providing the necessary bullshit to convince the business manager that I could perform the necessary duties.

The work was easy and I enjoyed working on the planes. I was making $4.00 per hour. My wife, Anne, was able to get a job at the local bank. We were doing ok.

Working on small airplanes gave me the desire to fly. By this time I had met many pilots around the airfield. The decision was made...I will learn to fly!

My first flight was in a Cesna 150 Aerobat. This means full aerobatic capabilities. My instructor was about thirty years of age. He had that look like if we died today, his life would be complete! Each day after work I would show up for my lessons. At night I studied the manuals to learn the art of pilotage.

Everything was going well. I could take off. I could land. I could even talk the aviation jargon. I could perform all of the numerous maneuvers and I performed the tasks just like a real pilot. After two weeks of flying I knew that I would never make a pilot! I did not feel safe nor was I comfortable in the air.

On the last day that I was to complete my training I

was given the thrill of doing a negative Gee-Loop. As my pilot, Jim, opened the throttle and the nose dropped, we were heading for the ground. I felt like I was in a dogfight with the "Red Baron". As the whistle of the wind increased, I figured that we were almost to mach one! As the instructor pulled up on the controls, my ass was as flat as a pumpkin that had been run over by a truck! The engine screamed. All loose objects in the plane were suspended in the air. As we climbed toward the sky I found myself weightless. "My God! I am in outer space!" As the plane continued to head for heaven, things slowly returned to reality. At this point, the plane had stopped in mid-air. The plane could no longer climb. There was only one direction it could go. DOWN!!! "Aw shit!"

Now we were flying backwards. Thinking that the nose of the plane would drop forward I soon knew I was wrong. The nose went up and we were tumbling backwards! "Aw shit!" As the plane fell over on its' back I could feel the blood in my head try to exit through my eyes. It seemed like five minutes. The plane rolled over and the ground was rapidly coming towards us. At this time I knew my life was over. I looked over to the pilot and he had a huge shit-eating grin of accomplishment spreading from ear to ear. He acted like this happened all the time, but to me, it seemed like an eternity. Well, we didn't die and soon we were safely on the tarmac.

After exiting the plane, the pilot asked me how I liked the roll. I said it was great and I couldn't wait to do it again. We walked into the flight room and I found out that I would go solo tomorrow. I was thrilled!

That night I lay in bed thinking about the big day. "To solo with the birds." Just the thought of flying in a plane all by myself scared me to death! I never showed up at that airport again! I quit my job and moved back to Seattle. "Home at last!"

Chapter 13

Anne's mom and dad were wonderful people. We were welcome to stay at their home for as long as it takes to find a job.

After making a few calls to some old bosses that I remembered from the big airplane company, I was able to land a position not unlike the one I had three years prior. Life is good!

As I was making good money building airplanes, I was always dreaming of other things. My wife, Anne, had also acquired a good job with the same company.

As things go, I became the proud father of my second son. His name is Raymond. Raymond and I were perfect! He was smart and I was too!

The house we had purchased had become better with extra effort from my wife and me. We lived in the house for seven years and I was always proud of the home that we had made. It had three bedrooms, a huge deck, a hot tub, and an in-ground swimming pool. We had numerous pool parties with friends and family. Work was going good and I was happy. I now feel cool! Life is great, but I am now having thoughts that life could be even better.

I am now no longer making tools at the airplane Company. About one year earlier I was given the opportunity to become an engineer and design the tools. This meant no more blue jeans. White shirt, tie, and slacks were in order. (I wish Dad could see me now!) Work today was very different than it was before. The people I was now working with were highly educated and spoke correct English. I felt completely out of place. I think they assumed that I was also educated so I figured that I would learn to talk just like them! Looking back, I cannot help but think of my mother from Muleshoe, Texas. She talked with a southern drawl and was always my inspiration to learn the English language. She would say, "Sound out the word and write it the same as it sounds." That was what I did then and still do today! I can barely spell my own name! (Hooked on Phonics!)

Things were happening so fast that I felt like we were traveling through outer space. Maybe we are traveling through outer space at twenty thousand miles per hour. I see a corporate galaxy speeding through the endless darkness of eternity. The planet is "Hope". All of the production activities are performed at "Ground Zero" where only first line managers and their producing subjects will reside.

"Hope" is a living planet and has an atmosphere surrounding it that can sustain life. There are many middle managers flying around in the "Atmosphere". They are over-seeing the activities of everyone at "Ground Zero" on "Hope". As we climb higher, we become weightless. Everything up there is free floating and orbiting the planet. The passengers in the orbiting vehicles are upper management. These managers are watching everything below.

Continue on and the space travel will finally take us to the star, "Hub". "Hub" is where we find the total rulers. (The CEOs', CFOs', and Board of Directors'.) The people on the planet dream of moving onto the "Atmosphere". The middle managers in the "Atmosphere" dream of moving onto "Orbit". The orbiting managers dream of a position at the star "Hub". The workforce dream of money and hope of someday getting off the ground.

The most memorable boss I ever had was recycled from outer space. He was very tall and was follicley challenged. Most of us young employees thought that he showed a striking resemblance to the cartoon character, Jimmeny Cricket. Sometimes we would also refer to him as O.H.M.E., or Onion Head Macho Engineer!

Jimmeny had worked his way from "Ground Zero" all the way to "Orbit". He was one of the very few that was ever recognized for his hard work and accomplishments. He reached his height of incompetence way before new age thinking had become the standard of today. He must have screwed something up, or ticked someone off from "Hub". I had always suspected that he may have been used as the fall guy for someone else's bad deed. Nonetheless, Jimmeny was in a decayed orbit and eventually fell back to "Ground Zero".

How fortunate we were to be able to tap into the complex mind of someone from outer space. He showed up with his pride in tact and managed with the grip of a seasoned Marine Drill Sergeant! He was God and we were his disciples.

Jimmeny and I clashed from the first day that we met. He knew everything and we knew nothing. A little training and reprimand was in order for his underdeveloped crew. On occasion, he would threaten to fire me and I would threaten to quit! One day I got so made at that S.O.B. that I told him that he should go and have sex with himself! He told me that I was very close to the end of my career. We didn't speak to one another for days. By the start of the fourth day he approached me and said that after not sleeping for three nights his guilt had over taken him and he wanted to apologize. I was glad and found comfort in his statement. To show my fairness, I also apologized to him. We both smiled and as he headed back to his office he whispered in my left ear, "Brent, please don't chew me out in front of the crew!"

After that day we became a real team and I had learned his compassion for me and other people. We became such good friends that we never passed up the chance to kid one another. He would say to me, "Brent, if bullshit was music, you would be a brass band!"

I would reply, "If brains were gasoline, you wouldn't have enough to run a piss ant's motor scooter!"

Months passed into years and everyone learned to love old Jimmeny Cricket. I was fortunate enough to get to honor him at his retirement party and M.C. the "roast". We had so much material on that clown that the party was a huge success! Even his wife and adult children enjoyed the fun.

He is now living the good life and if I had had my way he would have been returned to Orbit and beyond!

As the years are passing, my I.Q. is now going down and I must be getting dumber as I keep dreaming of bigger and better things. I wanted to play golf in the best Country Club in Everett. I suggested to my wife that we should sell our home and move to the town of Mill Creek.

The money kept coming in and I wanted a better and bigger house. At this point in my euphoria, I had already taken up the game of golf. As I was bored, it was an excuse to go somewhere on Saturday and not feel guilty. I had played enough to become a challenging contender. Now that I was becoming rich, I also wanted to be a WINNING golfer.

After days of my whining, Anne agreed to move to

this new place called Mill Creek. We held an open house and the first two groups of people wanted the place. We sold the house ourselves without a realtor. It only took us two more days to find our dream house on the reputable golf course. This placed called Mill Creek was like moving to Beverly Hills. After moving in, I joined the Country Club.

It wasn't long before I was hob-knobbing with the big shots of Seattle. Some of the members were stars on the local sport teams: Seahawks, Mariners and Sonics. My next-door neighbor was the Mayor of Mill Creek. Someone should walk up and slap my face! What a self-centered prick I was becoming. Later that year I won the club championship in golf. I won $2000 dollars. I must be ready to join the PGA!

My job was going well at the factory. Anne's job was doing even better. She worked a lot of overtime. I was free on weekends to play golf. In one year my handicap had dropped from a twelve handicap to a six handicap.

I usually played with the same group. We would meet for breakfast at the clubhouse. We would form a foursome and each deposit $50 bucks in the pot. Playing for money can get very expensive if you are a loser. When it came to golf, I rarely lost. The boys I played with were not very athletic and most were on the downward side of their game. This new life was great and also very expensive.

Six months passed and after hiding my old 1975 Chevy station wagon in the back corner of the clubhouse parking lot, I justified the purchase of a new 1986 318i BMW. I knew that this lifestyle would go on forever.

After eighteen months had swiftly passed I got the news that I will be single tomorrow. I guess golf just wasn't her thing.

My son and I stayed in the house and tried to continue as though nothing had changed. My golf scores started to go up and my interest in my job started to go down. By the passing of the second month of freedom I came to the realization that it was no longer in the stars to be "Jack Nicholas".

I listed the house with a realtor and kissed my $5000 dollar membership good-bye. Struggling for six months trying to manage the bills I was able to sell the house for a loss of $30,000 dollars!

Now my new lifestyle was becoming very similar to one of my old ones. Time heals all. Soon I was rediscovering my job and other people. I lost twenty pounds the first three months. I no longer looked like a "fat cat". I was beautiful again! When I was single I didn't need any food or sleep. I did a lot of hunting, but none in the woods. Now that I was no longer "Jack Nicholas", I had become "John Travolta"! I quit golf and started dancing. I even owned a pair of pants with buttons in the front. (Saturday Night Fever.) Some dancers may do better than others. I was so tired of being alone…I stopped playing hard to get!

Now that I am single and having sold my house on the golf course, I decided to move into a rental house. I thought that a house with a yard would provide a better environment to continue raising my young son. The house I would rent must be close to work and inexpensive. After one grueling hour of reading the "for rent" ads in the local newspaper, I circled the one that sounded just like the one I was looking for. I met with the owner and a deal was cut. She wanted a six-month lease. I, being a thinker, (fast at that!) knew that I should buy a new home of my own. I stopped renting twenty years ago and I was not going to be a renter for very long. The lease was signed with the agreement that I would purchase the next house of my choice through her. She, in turn, would release me from my lease contract if I agreed to buy ONLY from her.

Two days before the closing of the Mill Creek home, my son Raymond and I started moving our belongings into the rental house. After we had completed ten or so trips from one house to the other, we were becoming more and more fatigued. When my wife and I had started dividing up the household contents I felt that she was taking more than she should. Now, with the move becoming a major event, I had wished that she had taken even more!

After completing the last load, we were relieved. The move was finally complete and we were starting to settle in for our first night in the new digs. Darkness fell and we turned on the television. It worked fine. It was time for dinner. When I stood up to head for the kitchen I noticed that the white socks that I was wearing were now black! I could not believe my eyes! After a little more observation, I was able to deduce the cause of this phenomenon. To my shocking surprise, my white socks were covered with fleas! That night, Raymond and I slept in the bathtub.

The next morning as I awoke, I could barely stand up. The tub must not have been a very comfortable bed. In the light of the day I could not see anymore fleas. I guess fleas must be night people. With the speed of a three-toed sleuth, I slowly entered the shower. The warm water felt good on my sore body. With the shower complete, I started the redundant move of drying. "What are all those red spots on my legs? Flea bites!" That's what they were! Now I figure that I would get the bubonic plague! For some reason my son, Raymond, didn't have as much as one bite! Not wanting to spend one more squirming night in that house, I decided to call the landlord. Threatening to move out, I was told by her to get some flea bombs and eradicate the pestering guests. Since I knew that I didn't want to repeat the grueling task of moving again, I agreed to give it a try. Flea bombs were new to me, but after a trip to the necessary store I had acquired three bombs. I started setting them off: one in the living room and two in the bedrooms. Returning to the house three hours later, I slowly peeked my head into the house to see if I could see any survivors. The coast was clear. By the next day I detected a slight smell of dead animals. It must have been the fleas. After vacuuming the entire house I dumped the full bag from the machine. I had just captured five pounds of deceased fleas!

Work was going well. During my many years at the Company I was aware of an elite group of people. These people were the "swat team" of the aircraft industry. They were elite and notorious. With thousands of airplanes in service around the world, sometimes there would be a breaking news story of a catastrophic crash. Ninety percent of the incidents would involve the total destruction of the plane, crew, and passengers. Luck or fate, I was offered the opportunity to join the elite team that would investigate the destruction.

We hear of near misses and aborted take offs. These aborted take offs and runway mishaps can put the plane into severe danger. When one of these incidents would occur, the elite swat team would be put into action. Huge jet liners cost millions of dollars and a "fender bender" can also cost millions. Some of these planes were repairable and the swat team would go to the rescue. We would travel the free and un-free world to analyze and repair planes that had suffered a non-fatal mishap. This was a job that could remove team members from home for weeks at a time. Never was any prior notice given. We were directed just like the United States Military. Any crisis, anytime, leave tomorrow! My job was to travel to the location of the plane down and after careful inspection, make determinations as to the need of parts and tools required to bring the damaged bird back to profitable service.

Joining the crew was easy. Working with them was difficult. The members of this crew were in a world of their own. I, being the new member on the team, would have to prove myself. To join this group was like joining the motorcycle gang of the 1950's. (The Hell's Angels.) They had true leaders, they all stuck together, and a new member should not be trusted. The talent displayed by these exclusive characters never impressed me. Most were connoisseurs of nature's nectar and many displayed less than a clean, moral character.

On long trips that required international flights, we would usually fly first or business class. The on-board food was much different than that of which I was accustomed. I would be served pate (ground goose livers), sushi, and caviar. At dinner time one of the flight attendants would approach me and say, "Sir, which entrée from the menu would you prefer?"

I would respond, "I don't see it on the menu. Do you have bologna sandwiches?"

For accommodations we would stay in one of two types of hotels: Five star, or four star. The room prices could range anywhere from $160 dollars to $900 dollars per night. The Company paid regardless of the price.

Even though I was on a food allowance, I still had to manage my budget. In the hotels that I stayed in, the dining room food could be more expensive than I could afford. "Where is Mickey-D's?"

I completed many trips around the world and I eventually became one of the team. My travels enabled me to forget my past and seek adventure that most could only read in a fiction novel. I, in my most depressed days, have walked through the back dark alleys of Hong Kong, Singapore, and New Deli. I look back now and think that I must have been living in the twilight zone. The thought of the remote places I have walked scares me today.

I actually loved the many trials and tribulations of my travels with the "Hells Angels"! Maybe we were not the "best" people for the job, but there was no one else at that time that knew how to fix those planes! While I enjoyed the many travels I experienced, they were really just a break in my day-to-day routine of going to work five days a week.

It is hard to go through life without coming into contact with some that you often think of. When I was promoted to crew leader some time back, I was also introduced to a new boss. His name was Reggie Smith. What a wonderful guy! Reggie was a black engineer from New Orleans, Louisiana. He was only twenty-eight years of age and had been working as a contract tool designer for a couple of years before being hired directly into management. His newfound promotion would be a challenge for him. He would now manage my crew and me! His job responsibilities included the production of all airplanes on all lines. His transformation from sitting at a computer and desk all day to being responsible for what people do and taking the blame for being late would be a quick one. I would be his lead and my crew would become his future. On his first day he told me that he didn't know my job or responsibilities. I knew almost everything about how to make airplanes. He told me that if I would teach him the ropes of production, he would always go to bat for me...a promise that he kept years later. What a deal! Reggie was one of the best tooling design engineers in the industry and I was a little white boy from Bitterwater. He treated me like he had never met a white boy in his life. I was given unearned respect and he made me feel like I had something to offer. Wow! He was eager to get things going and I was too. I said, "We can work together and I will teach you my job and what my crew and I do." He, in return, said that he was very appreciative of my cooperation and we would become a proficient team. Time passed and we became very close in friendship and shared work ethics.

I remember one day when Reggie and I were boarding an elevator to the top floor of engineering. We stepped in and were soon joined by another member of our team. He was a short, red-haired engineer named Whitney Sam. Both Reggie and I were very familiar with Sam and we both liked him a lot. Sam, like Reggie, was from New Orleans and would be seen as the typical stereotype from the deep South. Sam would always talk fast and sometimes ramble. He was extremely excited that day and wanted to explain a problem that was going on in the factory. He began by saying that he was "informed by that colored boy down on the factory floor".... I stopped him in the middle of his sentence and asked, "What color was the colored boy?"

Sam, with a confused look on his face, said, "What are you talking about?"

I responded, "Well, I am pink, you are red, and Reggie is black! What color was the colored boy?"

Reggie laughed while Sam stuttered and stammered. I was embarrassed for him! Reggie took everything in stride. After all, he was a space traveler and Sam and I were not.

Chapter 14

I have never been very good at being single, nor married. When I was single, I was lonely. Up until now, I had always failed as a husband. I think that maybe I was always a good husband, just a lousy picker of wives!

Most of my friends were married with children. On occasional visits with these friends, after dinner the subject of me being single would always come up. My friend's wives always wanted me to meet and date one of their female family members, or divorced friends. I didn't date any of them! If I had dated them and, as more usual than not, the relationship would go sour, I knew that I could lose my friend. Besides, I dated many women who had been divorced, but I had never married one! Just to imagine what had occurred to break up their previous marriages; I couldn't help but think of them cheating on their husbands, screwing him out of everything, and moving the kids to another state!

I came up with the following rules that I would always follow.

The Ten Rules of Dating for Divorced Middle-Aged Men, by Brent Johnson

1. Never date the boss's daughter.
2. Never date your friend's sister.
3. Never date an ex-wife.

4. Never date anyone from work.
5. Never date a woman that is unemployed.
6. Never date a woman that earns ten times more money than you.
7. Never date a woman that lives with her mother.
8. Never date anyone that had just completed their fifth tour of Drug & Alcohol Rehab.
9. Never date a woman who has a son in jail.
10. Never date a woman that lives with a giant Labrador.

I have always followed my rules to a tee…except for once! All was going fine until one day. While investigating a small tool design problem, my life was about to change. I had been dispatched to a far, out of the way, Company building. As I entered the business office in the building I noticed a young and beautiful female sitting behind a desk quietly speaking on the telephone. I couldn't help but stare. After about one minute of watching her I felt myself blushing like a boy that had just been told that he had wet on the toilet seat and should grab a bucket and a sponge! She had momentarily looked over to me and smiled. My heart missed a beat!

The next day, I called that same building to talk with one of the managers. I asked to talk to one of my old friends and fishing buddies, Pierpont Wilson. While not wanting to give away my motive of the call, I asked if the design problem that I had fixed the day before was going ok. He said, "Yes, but why did you REALLY call?"

I said that I was curious about who that beautiful, young lady was sitting at the front desk.

With a smirk in his tone, he quickly informed me that her name was Michelle and she was twenty-four years old and single. "Forget that! Sounds like jailbait to me!" Besides, no woman that young and beautiful would want to date an old man of forty-two with kids as old as her!

Pierpont couldn't wait to set up a meeting of the sexes!

One evening after work I stopped, as usual, at one of the local pubs to visit with co-workers. We often did that so we could sit back, get half bombed, and tell each other how good we were and how stupid the boss was. To my surprise, in walked the lovely Michelle. I couldn't believe my eyes. Walking right behind her was my old friend, Pierpont. I thought that that old jerk must be dating that young, beautiful girl! "How disgusting! What could she possibly see in him?" Pierpont was old and only four years younger than me! After introductions were made, I observed the two of them and how they had responded to each other. It didn't appear to me that she was showing any interest in him at all. Now my interest in her escalated! I began speaking clearly to her and maintained a good ear as to what she was saying. I went home that evening still trying to figure out what Pierpont was doing with her. Although he was a good friend, I couldn't see the two of them together.

While there were many people that touched my heart at the big plant, one of the managers that I recall was quite proper. He had learned his style by growing up across the pond in England. His name was Seymour Willey. We think that Willey had entered the United States with some type of green card. Although when he spoke he sounded like James Bond, his appearance was more like that of the deceased actor, Dudley Moore.

These Brits liked to drink. One day after work we all stopped at the pub to down a few pints. After a few rounds of Guinness I couldn't help but notice that "James Bond" had just turned into the movie character, "Arthur"! I love to hear the British talk...especially with their intriguing accent. By the third round, "Arthur" was getting so drunk that he now sounded like he was from Scotland. Man, could he butcher the English language! Willey was always a gentleman and he was one of my favorite bosses.

A few days had gone by since my meeting Michelle when I was shocked with a phone call from her. She was inviting me to go out with her on a "real" date. I agreed while trying not to sound too anxious.

Not long after Michelle and I started dating, I had to break some nerve-wracking news to Willey. One afternoon I had made the quarter mile trek out to the truck after work where Michelle was supposed to be waiting for me. Instead, Michelle met me half way with the look of a cat about to get run over! I asked her what was wrong and she stated that she had just run my truck into a car in the parking lot when she turned too short. I asked her who the car belonged to and she replied that she didn't know, but it was a REALLY nice car! She had come to find me and didn't know if there were any witnesses. She led me to the damaged vehicle and to my horror, it was Willey's brand new, bright, shiny red, GT Mustang Convertible!

Being the honest person that I am, I trekked the quarter mile back to the office and cautiously approached "Arthur's" desk. He said, "What's up Johnson?"

I said, "You know all those beautiful, red cars out in the parking lot? Well, you'll now be able to tell which one is yours!"

He responded, "What the hell are you talking about?"

I told him, "Michelle just misjudged her exit from the parking lot and accidentally drove over the left front fender of your beautiful new sports car!"

After he gained some composure he became less concerned and all would be forgiven. Thank the stars for insurance!!!

Michelle and I have been together ever since our first date…even after she had wrecked my boss's car! We became man and wife fifteen years ago and to this day, she is my best buddy. We still spend all of our time together and I am now not only just "lucky", but I have also become a good "picker"! I still don't know what she ever saw in me.

After the wedding, Michelle told me that she was in love for the first time in her life. I said to her, "I am in love for the LAST time!" No longer an eligible bachelor and not having a worry about my friend's wives fantasizing about me, I would now put full effort into my work.

Once again things were going just a little too good for me. After one year of enjoying the security of married life, it was time to start dreaming once again of fishing, hunting, and outdoor adventures. When I made the suggestion that Michelle and I should quit our jobs and move to Montana she couldn't stop jumping with joy. I was thrilled…again!!!

The selling of the house was easy. The real estate market was booming and we would make a killing from the sale. It only took one week to find a buyer and we were able to avoid utilizing the services of a realtor. Prior to my meeting Michelle, I had purchased this house with a small down payment of only five percent. The down payment came from my reliable old pal called the "visa". We made a $40,000 dollar profit on that house in just two years. That was the only good business deal that I had ever made in my entire life! We loaded up what furniture and other household belongings that we could fit into a U-Haul trailer. We were off to the new promise land by way of Mexico. "On the Road Again!" (Willy Nelson.)

The trip would lead us to the southern tip of the Baja Peninsula, Cabo San Lucas. Michelle nor I had ever been to Mexico. We picked Mexico because growing up in California, through osmosis, I had learned to speak a fair amount of pigeon Spanish.

Once we arrived our search for a condo was disrupted by the cost. Condos on the beach were much more expensive than we felt we could afford. To save money we rented a condo back from the beach. This condo had beautiful, red tile floors and a view of the local residences. One problem with the condo was that it had no air conditioning. The temperature was so hot that not only could we not stand it, the cockroaches were carrying canteens! We had even signed a two-month lease, but when the landlord saw the sweat from my brow and the antagonism of my heart, she released us from the lease and we moved into a one star motel.

After a few days of strolling the beach and drinking my usual six-pack of Dos Equis, we decided to take a bus trip to the fishing village of La Paz. La Paz would be north, up the Gulf, one hundred and fifty miles. The bus was not a greyhound, nor did it have any luxuries at all.

We bought the $5 dollar tickets for the journey and proceeded to board the bus. As we approached the interior of the bus, we noticed that just like in the movies and the stereotype depictions of how things are on a Mexican bus, we knew that this was not going to be like any normal bus ride. To the left we could see a family carrying baskets with live chickens in them. Others were carrying baskets of produce. There was even a goat standing in the back! I looked around and I couldn't see a Caucasian on board. Suddenly the door slammed shut and the bus was off. The bus was full with the exception of two seats; one for Michelle and one for me. We couldn't even sit together. Being the gentleman that I am, I offered Michelle the choice of seats. She sat next to an elderly Hispanic lady and all was going to be fine. I cruised down the aisle and just before I stopped at the goat I spotted a vacant seat along the aisle. An elderly Mexican man had already taken the window seat. As I politely approached my seat, I looked over at him, smiled and said, "Buenos Dias." He must have been impressed with my Spanish because he smiled and gestured for me to sit next to him. I stored my luggage in the overhead and quickly fell into my seat. I was relieved! Wanting to recline for a little bit for the long journey, I flipped the lever with my right hand. The lever broke off and the back of my seat…including me…shot backward to a horizontal position! I now appeared to be in bed. While feeling comfortable in the reclined position, I couldn't help but hear the chuckle of a lady sitting in the chair behind me. I had just landed in her crotch and narrowly missed killing her chicken! I rode all the way to La Paz in that position!

At the halfway point, the bus pulled over in the middle of nowhere and everyone began exiting. It was lunchtime. Everyone bailed off the bus and headed for a one room outhouse to relieve themselves. To save time, many of the riders just walked to the back of the outhouse and relieved themselves in plain view. I decided that I did not have to "go" and Michelle said that she could wait.

The bus driver entered a grass shack with no windows. This was a restaurant. He sat at the table and a bowl of beans was immediately placed before him. He began to eat. We were getting pretty hungry but not seeing a kitchen, a sink, or soap we decided to just buy a coke and eat our packed bologna sandwiches.

Two hours later we arrived in La Paz, got a room, and spent the night. That evening we roamed the beach and had dinner in a very nice restaurant that was catering to tourists. The next morning we walked to the bus station and purchased another $5 dollar return ticket. The return trip was not the same road as the one we had taken yesterday. Instead, we had cut through the mountains and the scenery was very different. We were very concerned on whether or not we were really on the right bus that was going back to Cabo San Lucas. I couldn't help but worry about the condition of the brakes on that old rickety bus as we followed down miles of steep winding roads overlooking hazardous canyons. We felt like we were at Six-Flags riding the roller coaster of hell! We stopped once in a small village with a church. Next to the church was a pink, adobe building that displayed a sign over its' door. The sign read, "Mexican Food". We could never have guessed. We thought maybe they were serving lasagna! We felt as if we were in a Clint Eastwood spaghetti western. We didn't meet Father Hernandez, but we did see many donkeys and tipped sombreros shading the faces of siesta. Nightfall fell just as the bus was arriving at the recognizable spot of our journey's origin. At that point, Cabo felt like "home". After a month of walking the beach and swearing I would never ride a Mexican bus again, we figured we had better get our butts to Montana.

The plan was that we would live in the solitude of the country and only work when the need for money won over the thrill of freedom. We arrived in a place called the "Bitterroot Valley"…kind of sounds like the "Bitterwater Valley". It only took three days to find a small house on a one-acre plot. The house was in good repair and the mountain-view was spectacular. The decision to purchase this house was made and we soon moved in. From our residential vantage point, as far as the eye could see, we could take in the breathtaking view of the famous snow capped Bitterroot Mountain Range.

We would hunt game and fish for trout most everyday. Everything was good and even the garden was producing ample amounts of vegetables. Close to the house and in the backyard I was proud of the two huge cottonwood trees. A comfortable hammock stretched between their trunks where I would take my afternoon naps.

Now that we were alone in our new environment, it wouldn't be long before we started getting lonely and wanted to share our experiences with friends and family. We began extending invitations and soon company started to arrive and we were no longer lonely. We lived in the Bitterroot Valley for nine wonderful months and we were rewarded with company for eight of them! Life had become like a fairy tale and things seemed no different than living in a dream!

After the quick passing of nine months, the money started running thin. It was time to pursue employment! We could find minimum wage paying jobs, but we thought we could do much better. To do better we would now have to get "real" and move back to Seattle to boost the old bank account.

We knew that this dream chapter in our lives was over and so it was back to work we go. "Hi Ho, Hi Ho, It's Back to Work We Go!" (Snow White and the Seven Dwarfs.)

Chapter 15

Arriving back in the Seattle area we were the recipients of more good luck! Always being Mom's favorite, it was now time to collect more rewards. Dad had passed on a few years earlier and Mother had moved to Seattle where she met and married a wonderful man named Fred. Mother and her new husband were heading to Mesa, Arizona to spend the winter so that Freddie could play on a senior softball team. This trip would leave their residence vacant for a period of six months. With me, being the favorite AND needing a place to live, Michelle and I moved in rent-free. What a deal! Now it is time to make contacts with old friends at the former airplane company where we had just quit our jobs nine months earlier. I often think that some people are a little jealous of those that take a chance by giving up the security of their jobs and family. This jealousy can result in their wanting to help you after you have failed. Using this to our advantage, it was easy to get over them saying, "I told you so!"

Two phone calls later and Michelle had found her job. This position was the same as the one she had prior to our adventurous move to Montana. She is now a Human Resource Manager. Finding a job for me was not quite so easy. Maybe some of my old work cronies had thought that I had not been punished enough and that a few more years of missing my old job was what I needed. It only took me one week of sitting at home before I started to become a little more concerned. In those days I easily became paranoid and I usually over-reacted to everything. After receiving the next phone call, I was no longer concerned and I was once again back in the game.

When the phone rang I didn't recognize the voice on the other end of the line, but I was eager to hear more. The voice was a man and he began to inform me that I had been recommended by one of my old bosses and good friend, Reggie. The requirements of this job consisted of organizing and building a temporary workforce for the Company utilizing highly trained tool design engineers. These engineers would possess the skill to design aircraft components and tools utilizing 3-D computer graphics. The Company had just started designing for the production of a new large airplane.

The next day I reported for the interview and began fielding the questions thrown to me by my future boss. After being asked a few unrelated questions about airplanes, I realized that he had never designed a tool in his life. How to build an airplane was as boring to him as flight is to a lizard! He was a professional "architectural engineer". I will take advantage of his lack of experience and I would immediately shift into gear and baffle him with my brilliance. He went for me like a hog goes for garbage! I got the job and I would be earning more money than I had been when I ended my employment nine months earlier. There was even a promotion in the deal and I would feel like I was a real engineer too!

My new boss, Boyd, was nearing retirement age and

looked just like Sadam Hussein. He was the first boss I ever had that displayed gray eyebrows and coal, black hair. Looks like a dye job to me!!!

Michelle and I are back in the bucks again!

When I reported to work, I found out that I was replacing another man due to his announcement to retire. My new office was large and I now have my own secretary. The work area that housed my crew and me was located on the seventh floor of a towering building over looking the bustling Seattle-Tacoma airport. I felt like I was completely out of my element and that a crime had been committed. I was not a real engineer, but all of my recruits would be. The bosses that I was now involved with were extremely big thinkers and high rollers. They knew the "privileged few" of the Company by their first names. I am determined to fit in! With my first paycheck I went to Nordstroms and bought three new suits. I even bought a pair of Bruno Malley shoes. I was so cool that I told my secretary that she didn't need to call me "Mr. Johnson".

Now with the stage set, it was time to write the play. The boss that I had replaced had completely written the wrong script and his business plan was a shamble. He had ordered the wrong computers and hired the wrong talent. He was thinking in terms of low cost and low wages. He believed that he and the other architectural engineers were the "cream of the crop" and that tool design engineers were nothing but draftsmen.

125

Draftsmen are talented people, but they are not tool engineers.

No industrial product can be produced without the proper tools. A tool engineer must imagine how to fabricate and build the final product. In the aircraft industry, a tool could be a structure the size of an apartment building, or it could be as small as a matchbox. When we wake up in the morning and turn on the television we often witness the take-off of the space shuttle. All of the huge support structure next to the craft itself that doesn't leave the ground is "tooling".

Now that I have a new job, a small crew in place, and the business plan is complete…I need customers! I, with the help of my managing team leaders; Mike Cowlick, John Opinion, and Andy Woodpecker, were able to author and print a simple business plan which included what **services** we could provide. I had little control of the Company business so selling our skills was a must. After making a few contacts with other division managers we were given the opportunity, on a limited basis, to produce tool designs. My boss was thrilled to hear we had just signed on our first customer.

Our plan was to produce high quality designs, on time, and be competitive with the outside vendors. The Company had two options: It could design in-house, or hire outside vendors to provide this service that would prove to be more expensive. The business plan was a huge success and soon we became the number one tool design provider of choice.

Tool designers are only needed at the beginning of a new product. One tool will be used to make many hundreds of parts. Therefore, a tool designer often will design him or herself out of a job! Tooling is not taught in any college engineering classes. All tool design engineers learn their trade by "on the job osmosis".

At this glory time in my career I felt grateful for the opportunity I had been given by others. I was now in the position to return some of my good fortune to others. I executed a plan to provide training and opportunity to young students who were learning drafting. I notified a Vo-Tech school in Renton. I offered their drafting instructor the chance to provide me two of his top students. I would offer these selected students a career opportunity of a lifetime; my crew will teach them to be tool designers. The school was quick to respond and in a very short time interviews were arranged. I met a young man and one young lady that stood out from the other referrals. They reminded me of me when I was young. These two offered no bull and I offered each of them a job upon completion of their schooling. These kids showed up and both became top tool design engineers.

To this day there are only about two thousand aircraft tool designers in the world. These elite people, when needed, can demand a six figure salary; unlike architectural engineers that usually make $30 dollars per hour.

We now had acquired many customers from throughout the United States. At the peak, we were designing tools for commercial airplanes as well as helicopters, ships, and military fighter planes. We even did some work on the International Space Station.

My organization grew from a mere fifteen employees to a world-class team of one hundred and twenty-five designers. Even I was finally given that promised promotion. I am now in middle management and flying in the "Atmosphere"!

By the third year of operation, we had delivered over $50 million dollars of product to our customers. I had been voted by the Orbiting managers the title of "Manager of the Year" at the division level. I was at the height of my life! I love my job and I want this to go on forever.

After two years and with the new airplane far along into production, the request for new tools began to diminish. I was notified that my organization would disband. I will get demoted and will need another job. As a wise man once said, "No good deed goes unpunished!"

It takes a lot of time and even more hard work to create and build a good business. Dismantling only takes about one week.

I am now back on the ground and no longer flying in the "Atmosphere". I am now a first line manager and my new, small crew and I are on "Ground Zero". I no longer look up, but sometimes I can hear the planes pass over. My new dream may be my last dream. I have now lost all ambition to succeed. I am looking for the "golden handshake". I am doing what I must just to complete the daily tasks. "I miss Bitterwater!"

To pass the time, I would sit in my office and think of my experiences of the corporate world. What makes a manager and how do they become space travelers? I suspect that all managers start out with the idea that they will be fair minded and provide a real service to mankind. All first line managers start at "Ground Zero" and work their way up. Only five percent of these managers even get to the next level, "Atmosphere". Of the five percent now in middle management, only one percent of those will ever make it to upper management, "Orbit". None of these orbiting managers will ever make it to the star, "Hub".

I remember back when I was promoted to the position of a first line manager. I would become an overseer of people and what they produced. I was given the tools necessary to motivate them and keep the wheels turning. I really cared about their security and happiness. I tried to encourage good effort and promote Company pride. From the first day as a manager, the Company provided me with a hat. This hat had a long stick protruding forward, just out of my reach. At the end of the stick was a string. At the end of the string was the ever elusive yellow carrot! When I would see a middle manager stroll down the hall, I would watch his carrot dangle to his lumbering stride. It seemed like almost everyone was wearing that hat!

When I was young I was always chasing that carrot. In fact, almost everyone did! I did, however, notice that some of the older employees showed little interest in the run. They wouldn't wear the hat!

The Company spent a lot of time and money trying to inspire productivity through motivation and carrot chasing. We would attend classes and dream of more money and bigger jobs. I saw many people wear that hat and chase that carrot for thirty unsuccessful years. What stamina! Most of our new engineers were recruited right out of school. We only hired from the top Abet Accredited Universities. I myself had been on numerous recruiting trips. All of these young kids were ambitious and very intelligent. They would wear the hat without question. They were the best! Kind of reminds me of the fake ball throw to a dog and watching him run to retrieve the invisible object. Unlike people, a dog will only be fooled a few times!

The entire game was to rocket up the ladder of

success. At first, if you do not succeed keep on sucking and you will succeed. As the saying goes, "The only way to move up is to either marry the boss's daughter, or you could work very hard for twenty years and THEN marry the boss's daughter!" Most managers promoted others with the same criteria as they had been. Keep those that work hard working hard. Promote those that are loyal and agree with everything their boss might say! Even lie, if necessary, to protect the boss. Spying for the boss is also highly regarded. This system has been in place ever since the first cave man needed someone to do his bidding and is in full use today all the way to the star, "Hub". The only problem with this system is that many people get promoted to their height of incompetence. Kind of like "in-breeding". The more they multiplied, the worse it got! How the Company ever made any money is a mystery to me. Must have been those hard working, "Ground Zero" employees and first line managers!

The power of the Company only comes from the "Ground Zero" employees and a few of the managers flying around in the "Atmosphere". The value of the middle manager is to sometimes land and walk "Ground Zero".

About ten years ago, the Company began to listen to some spaceman that was orbiting "Hope". His idea was to recruit future orbiters and potential residents of "Hub" from the prestigious school of M.I.T. (Massachusetts Institute of Technology). These new graduates would become the dream team and managers of the future. The requirement and justification for pursuing these kids is that they would possess a B.A. in Aeronautical Engineering as well as an M.B.A. These pathetic kids could show up for work at anytime and become your boss. "God save the Company!" These kid's feet had never touched "Ground Zero" and never would. Most had possessed the shining, "silver spoon" from birth. Running down the aisle and throwing paper balls was part of their everyday job. Leave work early and forget to show up the next day was just fine.

I recall that one of my favorites was a young, tall kid that looked a lot like the cartoon strip character, "Dennis the Menace". Even though he was one of the young "privileged few", I really liked him and his humorous outlook on life. He never had a care in the world. On one day he told me that he liked hearing about how good I USED to be.

I replied to him, "At least I HAVE a past and a lot of experience and training! I like hearing about how good you are GOING to be!"

He said, "Well, that may be true, but at least I'm not fat!"

I replied, "You need to understand, I am NOT fat and this is NOT my regular job! I am actually a full time suma wrestler and if you give me any more of your shit, I will put on my diaper and kick your ass!"

We became good friends.

   It only took two years of throwing paper balls and
"Dennis the Menace" was off to "Orbit". Kind of like he
went back to outer space where he must have been from.
Dennis never wore the hat. He didn't need to chase the
carrot. Dennis WAS the carrot and I was too OLD to
chase him!

   The planet "Hope" was running like a fine Swiss
watch and airplanes were selling like rap music! It is
now time for the rulers from "Hub" to pay us a visit.
Things were going so well that these occasional visits
were necessary to make the employees at "Ground Zero"
feel that they were a part of the "big picture". The space
ship would exit the star "Hub", stop momentarily and
pick up a couple of the orbiting managers. Continuing
on, they would enter the "Atmosphere" and pick up a
few more middle managers. The space ship would
decrease its' speed and slowly land at "Ground Zero" on
the planet "Hope". With them, they would bring gifts
and awards to the fastest carrot chasers on the planet.
These gifts could include a hat with a SHORTER stick
and a BIGGER carrot. Coffee mugs were also highly
prized. These distant travelers would almost appear like
Gods. I think that some believed that they really were
God! The rules and even civil laws did not apply to
them. These people are so powerful that even the
President of the United States wouldn't want to get on
their bad side. I can't help but think of the many
companies in the news today, 2003. Not one ruler from

"Hub" has ever gone to jail...as of yet! After passing out the few hats and coffee mugs, these space travelers boarded the space ship and returned to their preset positions in space and time.

I don't know if working in a corporation is as fun today as it was then. When I was working, we were called a "big family". Now, employees are referred to as "the workforce". We used to be hired by "personnel". Now, people are hired by "Human Resources". Political correctness and harassment laws have changed everything.

I believe in Affirmative Action and I do not think that the young girls at work should be fair game for upper management. In the old days, managers would collect earrings (as I did in high school) but they kept them out of sight by placing them in their desk drawer. I didn't agree with this activity then, but I do believe that the definition of sexual harassment has been carried much too far! Women show up at work wearing short shorts. They may wear low-cut blouses to display the cleavage of their store-bought tits! This looks like an open invitation to take some kind of action! What if a man walked around with his pants unzipped and his "willy" partially peering at the scenery? Men are animals and their testosterone could influence their decisions.

The courts are full of harassment and discrimination cases. All of the people on trial are men! What we don't need in the workforce is more lewd women and more castrated men!

In the past, minorities and women were horribly discriminated against and maybe they still are. White men may have been the problem in the past, but the white working class men of today didn't cause it. There is no way to make up for the past injustices without hurting the present "privileged". I believe that everyone should be given an equal chance to acquire the brass ring and no one should ever get in their way regardless of race, color, or gender. To lower the ring for some is not fair and should not be part of the game. "Can't we all just get along?" (Rodney King.)

I have come to the understanding that we can all get through life with few scars as long as we accept that there are many "privileged" people throughout the world. I think that we "ground people" should "go with the flow, shut up, and get out of the way"! "Ground Zero" on "Hope" ain't that bad! If we can accept that, happiness will follow. It's ok to dream of outer space and "Hub", but if achieving all of our dreams is a route to happiness then many will be disappointed in the end.

Now that we have a basic understanding as to how business works and bosses are made, I will give you the dos' and don'ts of how to succeed in any job with any company.

No one ever got promoted to the next level without

possessing some ability to manipulate people…especially their bosses! Don't ever believe that your boss, or any boss got to their position because they were smarter than you or anyone else. If you weren't born of the "silver spoon", the number one requirement to get any promotion is to acquire a good mentor.

Follow the Brent Johnson rules of success and you too will be rocketed to outer space.

1. Acquire a mentor. Choose carefully.
2. Get the best education that money can buy.
3. From the first day of work, always be the first to arrive and the last to leave.
4. Do not become friends of any other employee that is lazy, or in any kind of trouble.
5. Avoid conversations with co-workers that like to talk about how stupid the boss is.
6. Learn whom the boss is screwing and leave her alone.
7. Remain neutral on your religious beliefs until you learn what religion the boss is. Join the boss's church.
8. If your boss is a Republican and you are a Liberal, don't pass up the opportunity to tell him how much you want to bomb Iraq.
9. If you discover that your boss is a loser and his boss knows it, transfer to another.
10. Volunteer to organize any work related projects.
11. When the hat goes around for someone that is either sick or dead, put $10.00 in the hat. This will be more than anyone else will contribute.
12. Ask your boss for his or her opinion as to what

after-hour classes you should take to be smart…just like him.

13. If you are married, have the boss over to your house for dinner. Your spouse needs to get to know your boss's better half.
14. Get to know your boss's boss and tell him that your boss is doing a really good job. This will get back to your boss and he will owe you a favor.
15. Find out what your boss does on his day off and make sure that is what you also do.
16. Volunteer to provide the donuts on Friday and save the cream-filled one for your boss.
17. On second thought, get two cream-filled donuts and give one to your boss and one to his secretary. This will encourage her to provide you with knowledge of where the boss is at all times and whom he's talking to (most important!).
18. Don't tell jokes about minorities or women.
19. Don't laugh about any jokes told about minorities or women.
20. Keep a copy of the Wall Street Journal on your desk at all times.

Congratulations! You now have all of the tools that you will ever need to board your rocket ship. One more word of warning: Don't collide with any other rocket ships on their way to outer space. By the way, if you have followed my rules to a tee and have not yet started to move up the Company ladder, then I would suggest that you marry your boss's boss's daughter!

Chapter 16

Planning for retirement is what everyone does. Just to get up in the morning becomes harder as the body starts to conform to the many shapes of stress. Everyone wants to believe that their plan is worth sharing with others that probably have a bad one. If you were me, you should do as I do and screw up every economical plan that has been put to work in the last five hundred years.

I wanted to retire twenty-five years before I was actually old enough. I didn't believe that I was actually even cut out for employment...just like Dad. Everyone at work was told from day one that they should start bi-weekly contributions from each paycheck to save for their future. I always made the maximum contributions. When the Company handed out the booklets to show everyone what was available for investments, the room was filled with fake interest and total confusion. Not many first time investors had a clue as to what the difference is between a blue chip stock or a small Company listed on the NASDAQ. I, however, was fortunate enough to have thought years ago that I would pursue a career in the sale of mutual funds and stocks.

In 1970 I had decided that I would become a stockbroker and become wealthy. I studied all of the material that I could find to understand what makes money for six months. Passing the NASD federal test was easy and after all of my studying, I learned that in order to buy a stock that will go up, you must first look at many tools to the trade. The Company prospectus, PE ratios, annual sales, acid test ratio, debt over liabilities, five year forecasts, new products and cost improvements, productivity of the work force…all of these tools sounded reliable, but later in my life I learned that they were total garbage.

Although I never worked as a stockbroker, I did invest a lot of money in the market. My problem was that when I got a few bucks ahead I would justify selling my stock and quitting my job.

My last nine years of working for the Aerospace Company, Michelle and I contributed to the Company 401K plan with the maximum allowed. For every $1 dollar invested, the wonderful Company would contribute .50 cents on our behalf. Even though Michelle and I really missed the money at the time, this was a very good deal. When I looked at my take home pay I was always depressed. Bi-weekly statements would read "earnings $2000". Sounds like big money. My deductions would read:

Federal Tax	$750
FICA	$121
UGN	$ 30
VIP	$175
	———
TOTAL	$1076

Let's see. To live on I now have $924 dollars to pay my household bills. ("I want Bush's tax cut!") It is one thing to feel rich, but it is another to realize that you are poor! Over this nine-year period Michelle and I were able to accumulate $200,000 dollars between us.

I was now fifty-five and couldn't wait to retire and just screw off. The Company would pay my lazy ass $1900 dollars per month for the rest of my life. In seven more years I would be eligible for $1300 dollars per month in social security payments. "Wow!!! This is almost as much as I had made chasing space people! Let's do it!" I retired and Michelle resigned.

Although Michelle and I had $200,000 dollars in our 401K plans, I knew that there was no way this money would last forty years. I also knew that there are a lot of tax laws governing any withdrawals before reaching age fifty-nine and one half. I figured that we would have to work part time and subsidize this "gold mine", but we were shocked! The stock market went crazy and everyday we became richer and richer. I could not believe my eyes. I would follow the market growth on my computer and dream of how high it will go. Within one glorious year, Michelle and I had now become wealthy. I couldn't wait to become as rich as Bill Gates! (One of the "Hub" residents!) I was drunk with the daily results of how much money we were making in the stock market. "Wow!!! If this keeps up, within two more years we will be worth $10 million dollars!" We had days of the stock market moving up to show a $20,000 dollar increase to our portfolio. It was unbelievable! "If this continues the money will be wallpaper."

The year 2000 rolled in and things started to look a little different. I remember watching CNBC, the stock channel. The world famous stock analyst, Abby, said, "The market is over-valued and there will be a ten percent correction." We were not concerned because we had made so much money that we could accept a "small correction" and time would be on our side.

Every morning Michelle and I would get up and turn to CNBC. Every morning they would offer guest speakers the opportunity to promote their agenda by lying about what the market has done, will do, and when it will recover. "What a bunch of crap!" The analysts would say that the market is "over sold and the **twenty percent** correction is just what the businesses need". I was so stupid that I was still happy because we had already made a fortune. "Where is the bottom?" The market went down and Michelle and I rode it! We were as stupid as a frog trying to cross a freeway. I had days of my gut wrenching. The government was telling us that we were in the best economy in the world and just hold on. What a bunch of liars these people were. Michelle and I lost $300,000 dollars in just one year! I could no longer stay the course! We are now very happy and broke! I don't believe anything I see or hear on CNBC.

I thought I was done with the story of my stupidity, but today I still have a little money left and I "day trade" on my computer. I believe that this stock market can go up just as fast as it went down. Dreams are what keep people happy and I will always have my dreams. My dreams are of better times and pride of accomplishment. I now understand why people believe in God.

Let's take day trading for example. If I can buy a stock for $1.00 and tomorrow I can sell it for $1.10, I must be profitable. That is exactly what I am doing today. I do not pay any attention to what their earnings are, nor do I give a crap about what any CNBC analyst thinks. I buy and sell by gut and play the game like I am in Vegas. This game is now fun and I am getting very good at being "on the road".

After all this I believe that President Clinton will have only two legacies in history. He will not be given credit for the best economic growth in U.S. history during any Presidential term. He was probably in the "right place and the right time". Maybe what President Bush Sr. did earlier was only rewarded later and Clinton got all of the credit. Who cares? The fact is that the stock market went up from 1993 to 1999 at unbelievable amounts and today we are where we are!!!

Chapter 17

I got a shot at the brass ring, but I was unable to hang on. The days of huge Company profits are becoming a thing of the past. Thanks to NAFTA (North America Free Trade), the competition is worldwide. Many of the big leaders of today will be knocked off their pedestals caused by the import of cheap labor and even cheaper products. Thirty years ago, the average person could hire into the same Company where Dad and Grandpa had retired. Those days are over. Few modern Companies now offer any retirement, compensation, or medical coverage and wages are down for the working class. Both man and wife must work outside the home to make ends meet.

The world is one pie. The United States, for the last one hundred years, has enjoyed most of it. The average stint of employment with one company lasts seven years. With the third world countries now entering the high tech global markets, our slice of the pie can only get smaller. Many of our industries are already gone and we are becoming a **service** providing society.

I did not get the "golden handshake", as I had hoped; but, I did get a Bronze one! I could have retired back in Bitterwater had I stayed, but on my last nostalgic trip to the old stomping grounds I witnessed a shock like that of being struck by lightening. To my surprise, Bitterwater, to include the quintuplet houses, had vanished from the face of the earth. Continuing up the road I observed that my one room schoolhouse, Choice Valley Elementary, was also gone. "Where is Mrs. Nuisance?" As I continued up the valley, I approached the town of Shandon. Even more unbelievable was that my alma mater, Shandon High, was also gone. I felt like I had been raised in a fictitious town somewhere in Scotland. I think, its' name was "Brigadoon".

With Bitterwater gone and no hope of changing my past or reliving my life over again, I have found the perfect place to spend my "golden years". Michelle and I are now living near a serene, small town in Northwest Montana. I will continue to write, pursue the outdoors and make replicas of Indian bows & arrows. I still look in the mirror and think, "Damn, I'm good looking!" My dreams have not abandoned me and I still get the urge to search for "the gold in them there hills"! (**AND THAT AIN'T NO BOLOGNA!**)

A note to the readers:

My story may give you the idea that I was not happy with my exciting career of building airplanes. If you do believe this then you could not be any further from the truth. I, most of the time, enjoyed my job and the people around me. I believe the Company and my superiors were fair and treated me with respect. I was able to ride the space ship much higher than my wildest dreams could have taken me. If I had to do it all over again, I would have finished my education, to include an M.B.A. at M.I.T. and tried again…maybe making it all the way to outer space!

www.ingramcontent.com/pod-product-compliance
Lightning Source LLC
Chambersburg PA
CBHW032026170526
45157CB00002B/863

9 781412 000109